This book is to be returned on or before the last date below.

-4. MAY ··9

Kirklees
L014920
due 31/10/05

U. Sunderland
due 18·12.07
ND 23042

U. S'land
due 12.6.09 ND 30424

Lowe, John

Britain and foreign affairs,
1815-1885: Europe and overseas

HARTLEPOOL BOROUGH LIBRARIES

D1424632

IN THE SAME SERIES

General Editors: Eric J. Evans and P. D. King

Britain and Foreign Affairs, 1815–1885

Europe and Overseas

John Lowe

London and New York

First published 1998
by Routledge
11 New Fetter Lane, London EC4P 4EE

Simultaneously published in the USA and Canada
by Routledge
29 West 35th Street, New York, NY 10001
© 1998 John Lowe

Typeset in Bembo by
Ponting–Green Publishing Services, Chesham, Buckinghamshire
Printed and bound in Great Britain by
Page Bros (Norwich) Ltd

British Library Cataloguing in Publication Data
A catalogue record for this book is available from
the British Library

Library of Congress Cataloguing in Publication Data
Lowe, John, 1934–
Britain and Foreign Affaris, 1815–1885: Europe and
overseas / John Lowe
p.   cm. – (Lancaster pamphlets)
Includes bibliographical references.
1. Great Britain–Foreign relations–19th century.
2. Great Britain–Foreign relations–Europe.
3. Europe–Foreign relations–Great Britain,
I. Title.   II. Series
DA530.L67   1998
327.4104–dc21   97-27212
CIP

ISBN 0-415-13617-2

Contents

Foreword

Lancaster Pamphlets offer concise and up-to-date accounts of major historical topics, primarily for the help of students preparing for Advanced Level examinations, though they should also be of value to those pursuing introductory courses in universities and other institutions of higher education. Without being all-embracing, their aims are to bring some of the central themes or problems confronting students and teachers into sharper focus than the textbook writer can hope to do; to provide the reader with some of the results of recent research which the textbook may not embody; and to stimulate thought about the whole interpretation of the topic under discussion.

Time Chart 1 Castlereagh and Canning 1815–1827/30

Foreign Secretary: Castlereagh (1812)

Prime Minister: Liverpool (1812)

1814	Ty of Chaumont.	Napolean surrenders 1st Ty of Paris (May)	Vienna Congress
1815	Hundred Days. Waterloo.	2nd Ty of Paris (Nov)	Vienna Treaty (June) Holy Alliance (Sep)
1818		CONGRESS OF AIX LA CHAPELLE (Sep–Nov)	
1819			Carlsbad Decrees
1820	Revolts: Spain (Jan)	Portugal (Aug); Naples (July) CONGRESS OF TROPPAU (Oct–Dec)	Troppau Protocol (Nov)
1821		CONGRESS OF LAIBACH (Jan–May)	Greek Revolt

Timeline 1822–1830

1822	French Invasion of Spain (Apr) · CONGRESS OF VERONA (Oct–Dec) · Chios massacre
1823	Monroe Doctrine (Dec)
1825	
1826	British Troops to Lisbon · d. of Tsar Alexander · Egyptian troops to Morea
1827	Ty of London (July) · St Petersburg Protocol (Apr) · Navarino (Oct)
1828	Russo–Turkish War
1829	Ty of Adrianople (Sep)
1830	July Revolution in Paris

Foreign Secretaries / Prime Ministers:
- Canning
- Canning Apr–Aug
- Wellington Jan
- Aberdeen June
- Grey Nov
- Palmerston

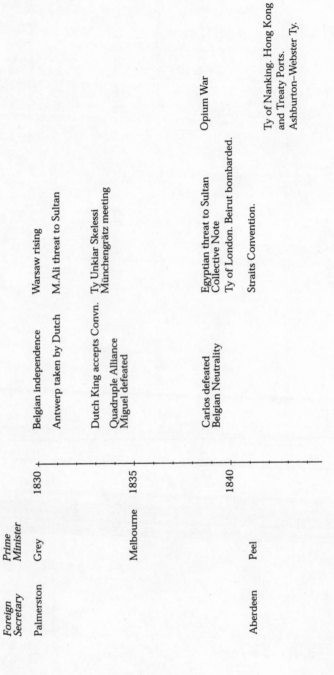

Time Chart 2 The Palmerstonian age 1830–65

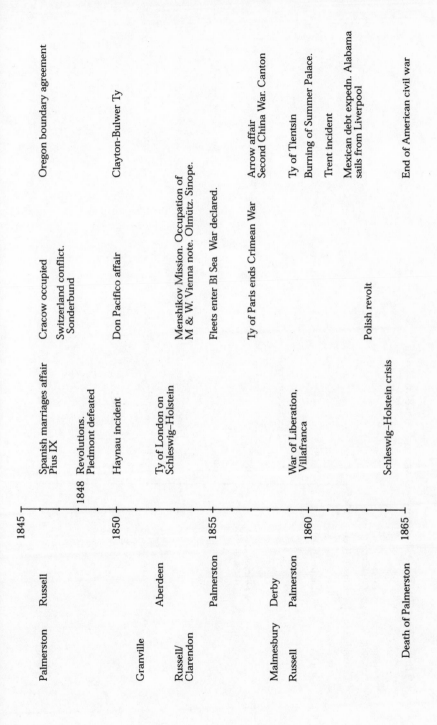

Timeline 1845–1865

Dates: 1845 · 1848 · 1850 · 1855 · 1860 · 1865

Events:
- Oregon boundary agreement
- Spanish marriages affair. Pius IX
- Cracow occupied
- Switzerland conflict. Sonderbund
- 1848 Revolutions. Piedmont defeated
- Haynau incident
- Don Pacifico affair
- Clayton-Bulwer Ty
- Ty of London on Schleswig–Holstein
- Menshikov Mission. Occupation of M & W. Vienna note. Olmütz. Sinope.
- Fleets enter Bl Sea War declared.
- Ty of Paris ends Crimean War
- Arrow affair Second China War. Canton
- War of Liberation, Villafranca
- Ty of Tientsin
- Burning of Summer Palace.
- Trent incident
- Mexican debt expedn. Alabama sails from Liverpool
- Polish revolt
- Schleswig–Holstein crisis
- End of American civil war

Foreign Secretaries / Ministries:
- Palmerston — Russell
- Granville
- Aberdeen
- Russell/Clarendon
- Palmerston
- Malmesbury — Derby
- Russell — Palmerston
- Death of Palmerston

Time Chart 3 The Gladstone–Disraeli Era 1866–1885

Foreign Secretary	Prime Minister	Year	Events
Clarendon	Russell (Oct)	1865	
Stanley	Derby (June)	1866	Austro-Prussian War
		1867	Luxembourg crisis
Clarendon	Disraeli (Feb) Gladstone (Dec)	1868	
		1869	Suez canal opened
Granville		1870	Franco-Prussian War; Sedan (Sep)
		1871	German Empire proclaimed; Black Sea crisis (Nov)
		1872	Alabama award; London Conference (Jan)
Stanley (Derby)	Disraeli	1874	

Year				Ministers
1875	Suez purchase		Bosnian revolt	
1876			Bulgarian atrocities	
1877	Transvaal annexed	Russo-Turkish War	Fall of Plevna (Dec)	
1878		Russians at Kabul	San Stephano Ty / Congress of Berlin (June)	Salisbury
1879	Isandhlwana defeat	Kabul massacre		
1880		Relief of Kandahar		Gladstone / Granville
1881	Majuba Hill / Pretoria Convention			
1882	Egyptian crisis / Tel el Kebir (Sep)			
1884	Sudan crisis	Bismarck's colonial demands	Berlin Africa Conference	
1885	d. of Gordon (Jan)	Penjdeh crisis	Bulgarian crisis 1885–7	Salisbury (June) (For Sec & PM)

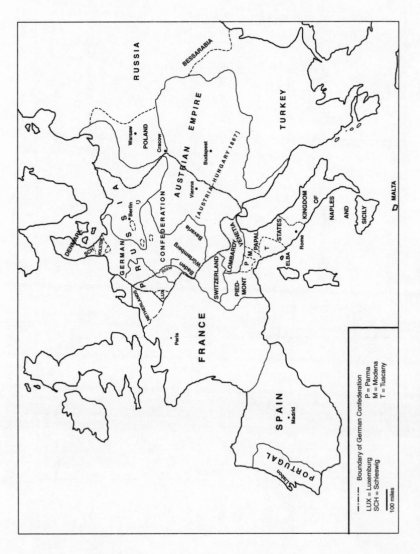

Map 1 Central and Western Europe in 1815

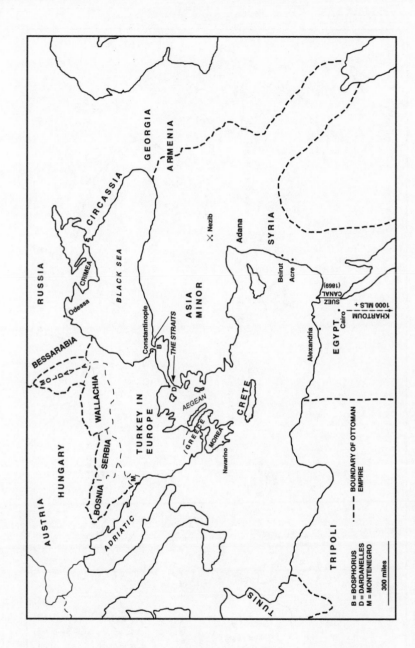

Map 2 The Ottoman Empire *c* 1815

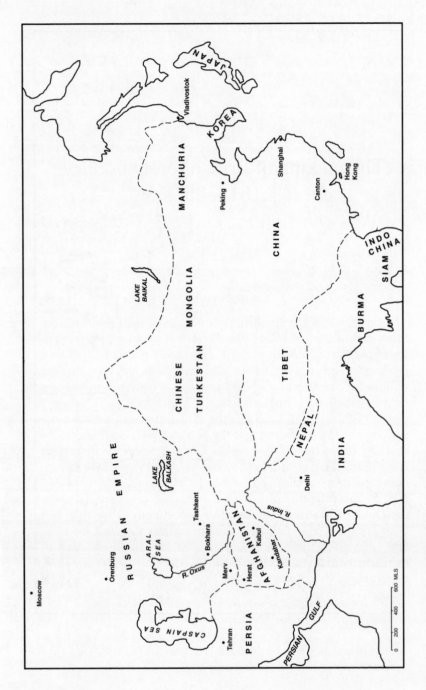

Map 3 Central Asia and the Far East

1
The making of British foreign policy, 1815–85

Introduction

The portrayal of the English as 'a nation of sea-farers' was an illusion, but the mere fact that Britain is an island situated at the edge of the continent of Europe has had a profound influence on her foreign policy. At its simplest, it meant that Britain, unlike her neighbours, seemed to have a choice – to become actively involved in the affairs of the continent or to adopt a posture of 'isolation' from Europe. The latter was not always a genuine choice. In the reign of the Hanoverian kings from 1714 to 1837 the defence of the royal homeland was an important issue. But Hanover apart, allowing Louis XIV or Napoleon to dominate most of Europe could seriously damage British interests. To meet the threat, Britain contributed large armies under the Duke of Marlborough and later, Wellington. The fact that both French monarchs made plans to invade England (in 1692 and 1805) highlights the importance of her island situation to her security. 'Having the sea for wall' a Tudor statesman put it, anticipating Shakespeare's verse:

> This fortress built by Nature for herself
> Against infection and the hand of war;
>
> . . .
>
> This precious stone set in the silver sea
> Which serves it in the office of a wall,

1

Or as a moat defensive to a house,
Against the envy of less happier lands.

Richard II, Act II, Scene I

The sea proved a better defence against French armies than the barrier fortresses of the Netherlands, providing, of course, that the navy was strong and kept in a seaworthy state – no mean task with wooden sailing ships.

Financing a powerful fleet (such as the 120 ships of the line in the 1750s) helped to push up the national debt from £14 million (in 1700) to £700 millions in 1815. The burden, however, was made easier by the growth of overseas trade, whose protection was one of the navy's major tasks. Hence the insistence in the 1750s that 'trade and maritime force depend upon each other'. If, in some of the seven Anglo-French wars between 1689 and 1815, Europe was the main theatre of war, in others colonial and commercial objectives were more prominent. This is a reminder that well before the Industrial Revolution, Britain traded with the American colonies, the West Indies, West Africa and India, as well as Europe. Regulating this trade was designed to create a trade surplus – 'the riches which are the true resources of this country depend upon its commerce' (**8**, p. 146). These 'riches' were the the essential sinews of war, not only in the competition for empire but also for hiring mercenaries or for subsidies to allies on the continent.

The interdependence of overseas and European issues was recognised by a French statesman in the 1760s when he said: 'In the present state of Europe it is colonies, trade and in consequence sea power, which must determine the balance of power upon the continent.' Priorities, or perceptions, could change, of course. It may have been the further growth of Britain's overseas trade and commitments that led her foreign secretaries a century later to assert that British interests were not involved in continental conflicts.

Continuity and change

From 1815 to 1865 continuity is a more dominant theme in British foreign policy than change. Thereafter, at least for the next two decades, policy changes seem to occur quite frequently. To some extent, of course, continuity is a matter of emphasis, a question of perspective, but in this case, personalities also played a part. The long 'Palmerstonian age' from 1830 to 1865 was followed by the era of Gladstone and Disraeli, whose views on foreign affairs had little in common.

Palmerston asserted in 1835 that 'England's interests continue the same let who will be in office.' It is far from certain that he would have made such a comment thirty years later, having witnessed Lord Aberdeen's markedly different perception of Britain's interests, as well as chafing at his view of how best to promote or defend them.

In defining her relations with other states, Britain's foreign secretaries naturally gave prominence to questions of security and strategy. Even so, relations could be affected by harmful restrictions on British trade. Foreign secretaries rarely seemed to expound a coherent set of ideas that might represent the principles on which British foreign policy was conducted. However, a few basic principles can be deduced which were valid for much of the nineteenth century: the desire for peace; the expansion of world trade; concern over the 'neutrality' of the Belgian coastline; and resistance to the domination of the continent by a single power (1).

The latter was usually the objective behind concern for the maintenance of the balance of power, which seems to have been a widely accepted if ill-defined concept for much of the nineteenth century. Until the 1860s, no major change in attitudes towards it took place, but the change then affected both parties more or less simultaneously. In 1814–15, Castlereagh's efforts to set limits to Russia's territorial gains, while balancing Austrian gains in Italy against Prussia's in Germany, contributed to the creation of that 'just equilibrium' which was conducive to stability in Europe. Canning's unease at the grouping of the Holy Alliance powers after 1820 was later shared by Palmerston, who claimed to have created a 'counterpoise' to it by an alliance of four western states in 1834. This East–West divide implied an ideological aspect to the balance of power but, in practice, the division was far from rigid. Being 'a system of practical mediation', as Palmerston called it, one of its virtues was flexibility, so its denigration in the 1860s by Cobden as a 'foul idol' was unjust. The Liberal Alliance of Britain and France from 1830 to 1846 was a shaky affair indeed, and ironically it was the Tories (Peel and Aberdeen) who fostered the *entente cordiale* more than Palmerston. In 1848 when the balance of power seemed threatened by the shock waves of revolution, spreading from Paris throughout Europe, Britain (as well as Russia) seemed to give priority to the restoration of stability (**2A**).

The main upset to the balance of power followed Russia's defeat in the Crimean war in 1856 and her self-imposed withdrawal from an active role in European affairs. Napoleon III's attempt to capitalize on this by trying to create a French diplomatic ascendancy in Europe caused some alarm to Britain's politicians (Palmerston excepted) but neither of the parties showed much concern at Bismarck's much greater challenge to the *status quo* in the late 1860s. On the other hand in 1871 the Conservative leader, Disraeli, was quick to grasp that the existing balance of power had been entirely destroyed by Prussia. The creation of a powerful military state in the centre of Europe produced a different response from the Liberal and Conservative leaders. Whereas Gladstone placed exaggerated hopes on international cooperation, through the Concert of Europe, the Conservatives came to rely on trying to win Germany's goodwill to resist threats to British interests.

'Non-intervention' was also an imprecise concept but its virtues were proclaimed in speeches in the House of Commons, when for example, Tories disapproved of aid being given to liberal regimes abroad. It also meant non-interference in the internal affairs of other states, but even this ideal was not always honoured. Meddling in the politics of the Iberian peninsula for several decades did not prevent British ministers from paying lip service to the concept of non-intervention before 1855 (**2D**, pp. 54–9). In the 1860s it came to mean not intervening in European affairs. Gladstone's desire to avoid 'needless and entangling engagements' was quite restrained compared to most of the 'Euro-sceptic' utterances of the post 1865 period, which recoiled from the 'sanguinary muddle of Continental diplomacy' or dangerous obligations to 'Great military and despotic powers'. In 1875 the Earl of Derby (formerly Lord Stanley), Disraeli's foreign secretary, claimed that 'the policy of non-intervention in general in continental disputes is the one which finds most favour with the people of this country' (**29**). The notion that Britain should remain aloof from European affairs certainly seems more evident in the 1860s

4

than in previous decades. This was in part an understandable reaction to the sense of military failure in the Crimean war of 1854-6, the perceived futility of which was such, *The Times* asserted even as late as 1861, that 'Never was so great an effort made for so worthless an object.' It also stemmed from a recognition of Britain's powerlessness when large armies were on the march.

The Concert of Europe was another imprecise ideal that influenced some British foreign secretaries in the nineteenth century. In fact, despite the assertion by Muriel Chamberlain that 'Britain's role in the settlement of European affairs was often peripheral' in the period 1815 to 1871, Britain played an active role in European affairs during most of the forty years after Waterloo (**12**, p. 7). Even Canning, who refused to work within the Congress System, cooperated with France and Russia over the Greek revolt. Here again the Crimean war was a watershed, influencing Russia's policy as well as Britain's and reinforcing an existing trend towards a global rather than a European outlook.

Attitudes to empire

The issue of continuity in British imperial policy is in some respects linked to the problem of defining the meaning of imperialism. In 1815 the British Empire consisted of a disparate collection of territories, controlled from London, including Canada, parts of 'Australia', India, the Cape, and numerous islands in the West Indies. In the following decades, however, Britain's influence was extended well beyond this 'formal' empire by the growth of her trade throughout the world, creating what has been called 'informal empire' or 'creeping colonialism'.

Changing attitudes to empire have become difficult to pinpoint with confidence as standard interpretations come to be modified in the light of new evidence or approaches. The traditional view, elaborated in the works of Bodelson and Schuyler in the 1920s, held that 'anti-imperialism' was a widespread sentiment among political leaders and the public in the middle years of the century. In the 1870s or 1880s, by contrast, it was replaced by the 'new imperialism' of territorial annexations, especially in Africa (**7**, **6**).

Anti-imperialism had a logic to it. The action of the American

5

colonists in throwing off their allegiance to the crown in 1776, led to the conviction that colonies would inevitably seek independence from Britain as they matured. The revolt of the Spanish colonists in South America in the 1820s also seemed to confirm Britain's own experience. This disillusionment with colonies on political grounds was reinforced by the discovery that trade between America and Britain actually increased after the colonists gained their independence in 1782. This made a nonsense of the whole system of regulating colonial trade in the interests of the mother country. Experience therefore seemed to prove Adam Smith right. In his *Wealth of Nations*, published in 1776, he had attacked the restrictive legislation (such as the Navigation Acts) of the 'Old Colonial System' in favour of the principle of Free Trade, which finally triumphed in Britain with the repeal of the Corn Laws in 1846. For some decades before this, however, colonies seemingly continued to be regarded as a useful asset.

In mid-Victorian times, by contrast, colonies came to be seen as financial liabilities – 'millstones around our necks'. Even the smaller colonies like New Zealand were deemed 'wretched burdens which in an evil hour we assumed', since the costs of their administration (and defence) fell on Britain. Hence talk of the possible 'separation' of the colonies from Britain, especially by doctrinaire spokesmen of the Manchester School of *laissez-faire* economics. In 1865, a Select Committee Report looked forward to 'our ultimate withdrawal' from the coast of West Africa. The years 1868 to 1870 supposedly saw 'the climax of anti-imperialism'.

The few colonial enthusiasts of the period were a small band of Radicals such as Lord Durham (famous for his Report on Canada in 1839) and Gibbon Wakefield, who advocated 'systematic colonization' of Australia and New Zealand. It seems that emigration contributed to a change of attitude towards colonies of white settlement, which were readily granted self-government in one form or another in the 1850s. Another factor was the growth of the economies of the larger colonies and the expansion of trade with India, so that some parts of the empire came to be more highly regarded in time. Distinctive party political attitudes to the colonies are not very much in evidence. Some prominent Whigs, including the third Earl Grey and Lord John Russell, were well disposed towards them, partly on the grounds of prestige and power politics, but Palmerston showed little interest in the empire, apart from India.

In the 1880s the idea of empire seems to have caught the popular imagination. The daring deeds of explorers and missionaries in opening up the so-called 'Dark Continent' may have had some influence, together with the growth of colonial and commercial rivalry among the great powers. If Disraeli made imperialism almost the preserve of the Conservative party, Gladstone's well known anti-imperialist stance, influenced by the expense and immorality of colonial wars, seems to stand in contrast to it.

The fact that territorial acquisitions, especially in Africa, were a feature of the 'new imperialism' of the 1880s appears to offer a contrast with the idea, prevalent in mid-Victorian times, of relinquishing colonies. But, as many historians have pointed out, far from giving up colonies, governments of the earlier period made numerous additions to the British Empire, such as Singapore, Aden, Hong Kong, and Lagos, as well as large parts of India.

The historical debate over continuity or discontinuity in British imperial policy and in public attitudes to empire in the course of the nineteenth century has become ever more complex. This is partly because the evidence itself is quite conflicting and the differing interpretations of it almost endless.

One of the most controversial suggestions of the last forty years has been the concept of 'the imperialism of free trade', summed up as 'trade with informal control if possible; trade with rule where necessary'. Robinson and Gallagher used this concept to explain the growth of 'informal' empire, which supposedly embraced independent states such as Argentina, said to be in an unequal and dependent (and therefore imperialistic?) relationship with Britain (7, p. 24).

The case for continuity does not rest solely on Robinson and Gallagher's 1953 thesis (favoured by Cain and Hopkins). More recently, other historians such as Eldridge have presented evidence that undermines part of the case for discontinuity. This consists partly of disavowals of the alleged anti-imperial attitude of the mid-Victorian period and partly of evidence of a widespread consensus that Providence lay behind the expansion of the British Empire. For example, the Radical J.A. Roebuck insisted in 1849 that 'The people of this country have never

acquiesced in the opinion that our colonies are useless . . .',
even if they were unsure why colonies served a useful purpose.

That an ingrained pride in empire (parts of which dated back
to 1763 or earlier) persisted through the nineteenth century
seems perfectly credible. Even Gladstone conceded in 1878 that
'the sentiment of empire may be called innate in every Briton'.
Planting 'the seeds of freedom, civilization, and Christianity', as
Huskisson put it in 1828, made the authority of the British
Crown 'the most powerful instrument under Providence, of
maintaining peace and order' in many regions of the world, in
the view of Earl Grey in 1853. Similar sentiments can be found
in the comments of prominent men in the 1860s and 1870s and
presumably inspired the remark by Gladstone in 1881 that
'while we are opposed to imperialism, we are devoted to
empire'.

The British Empire was seemingly more loved by Britons than
its detractors allow. It meant more than just the profits of trade
and investment. It involved duties and obligations, a sense of
mission or trusteeship, and for that reason, Eldridge concludes,
the empire received the almost universal support of the Victorian governing class. Even Cain and Hopkins suggest that the
'imperial mission was the export version of the gentlemanly
order' and see the empire as 'a superb arena for gentlemanly
endeavour' (5, p. 34).

Socio-economic factors

By mid-century Britain had become 'the great Emporium of the
commerce of the World' according to Cain and Hopkins. However, the link between politics and trade is not as clear-cut as
might be expected. For one thing, Middleton asserts that 'few
decisions in foreign policy reflected merely trading interests'
which, together with manufacturing interests, received only 'an
occasional fleeting glance'. It may well be the case that in this
period 'Industrialists were not at the centre of economic policy
making,' as Cain and Hopkins maintain, but Middleton's views
appear to underplay the vital importance of trade and finance
to the growth of British power and global influence, after 1850
at least. Porter's belief that Britain's foreign policy from the
1850s onwards was firmly rooted in her economic situation
seems more acceptable, but he also admits that it was only very

rarely that the Foreign Office did anything more positive than remedy injustice to assist the growth of British commerce (**32, 5, 6, 9**).

The emphasis on 'gentlemanly capitalism', (Cain and Hopkins's description) as a major factor in Britain's rise to pre-eminence, offers a new approach. They argue that the key agencies in the growth of the British economy were not so much manufacturers as trading companies, financiers (especially merchant bankers), and professional agencies such as insurance firms and lawyers concentrated in the City, whose links with the personnel of politics and government were likely to be much closer. With the Bank of England playing an intermediary role between politicians, officials and financiers, the defence of Britain's overseas trade and other legitimate commercial activities was a perfectly proper concern of ministers. Indeed, Palmerston asserted that 'It is the business of government to open and secure the roads for the merchant.' In 1860 he made the point even more bluntly when he wrote: 'trade ought not to be enforced by cannon balls, but . . . trade cannot flourish without security'. What ministers recoiled from was playing the role of 'sheriff's officer', as Lord Salisbury termed it, when greedy private or corporate investors got their fingers burnt in questionable financial operations overseas.

British capital was being exported at the rate of £30 million a year as early as 1850, rising to £75 million by 1875, which yielded dividends of £50 million. By about 1860 Britain was responsible for 40 per cent of the trade in manufactured goods, producing over half the world's supply of coal, iron and steel, and cotton cloth. Hence Kennedy's suggestion that Britain was a different sort of power from her rivals in Europe. By 1850, for example, the whole of the continent was less industrial than Britain alone, whose economy went on expanding for a further twenty years. This suggests she was not just the 'warehouse' of the world, as Cain and Hopkins assert, but the 'workshop' as well (**8**).

Because the value of the pound was linked to a fixed quantity of gold (the gold standard) for which it could be exchanged on demand (convertibility) sterling became a world currency (long before the days of American Express). This made London the centre of the world's banking and insurance system, controlling shipping lines that regulated over one third of the world's merchant marine. Hence the assertion by Cain and Hopkins that 'commerce and finance were the most dynamic elements in the nation's economic thrust overseas'.

This leads them to challenge many of the conventional views about the impulses behind British imperialism. In their view, it was 'the rapid growth of services' fostered by 'gentlemanly capitalism' that explains 'the peculiar nature of British overseas expansion' (5, p. 12). This makes for a greater focus on colonies of white settlement, where British influence was strongest. It also suggests that the territorial acquisitions of the later nineteenth century (such as in Africa) were related to the continuing growth and success of gentlemanly capitalism, rather than to the failure and decline of manufacturing industry. The usual view that British policy was a defensive reaction to foreign competition and tariffs, exemplified by Porter's comment that 'imperialism was for Britain . . . a symptom and effect of her decline in the world, and not of strength' is thereby turned upside down. Given the complexity of imperialism as a topic, this stimulating reappraisal is likely to be regarded as somewhat controversial for some time to come.

Awareness of Britain's global pre-eminence seemingly made public opinion responsive to assertive foreign policies during the later Palmerstonian age when, Chamberlain suggests, 'The British public did believe that Britain held a unique position in the world,' or even that Britain had become a super-power, not just a world power (12, p. 6).

Relations between 'the first liberal and mature capitalist polity' and the rest of Europe were almost inevitably complicated by the marked disparity between them in both economic and political development. At the heart of Britain's relations with the continental powers from the 1850s onwards there lay a paradox. On the one hand Britain led the world as a trading and industrial nation, but the very strength she derived from this could not easily be converted into war potential. Changing patterns of trade also meant that Britain was 'drawn inexorably away from Europe' and towards an 'internationalistic' foreign policy, using her naval power to act the role of world policeman (8, 9). In Palmerston's view there were no better 'peace-keepers' than 'well-appointed three-deckers' (well-armed ships of the line). At the same time Britain was weaker than many of her continental neighbours, especially in military terms, because of the very nature of her economy and society, 'the kind of nation she was'. If it was the unique combination of prosperity with personal and economic freedom that distinguished Britain from the other European states, this same uniqueness could not have survived an attempt to create a continental style army to meet the challenges of the 1860s.

Military factors

Dependence on imports of food and raw materials meant that 'our only sure policy is to strengthen our fleet' as Rosebery said in 1894. Naval supremacy was vital to the defence of sea lanes around the world, as well as the best guarantee of security from invasion for the British Isles. Although Britannia's reputation as a great naval power persisted through the nineteenth century, the margin of superiority over her rivals sometimes seemed alarmingly narrow.

Economies in the years after 1815 drastically reduced Britain's massive warfleet of over 200 ships of the line and 800 'cruisers'. In the post war period funds were available to keep 100 big ships in seaworthy condition and adequately manned (a crew of 1000 apiece being needed). For a great commercial and imperial power, Britain's naval policy was, according to Bartlett, strangely haphazard (28). The naval high command failed to provide an appropriate directing intelligence, partly because most of the 200 admirals were incompetent or dotards. Manning was unsystematic, while gunnery was often a hit and miss affair (usually the latter). Improvements did take place and other fleets were often worse still, so that in relative terms the Royal Navy was strong. The Mediterranean Fleet, for example, gave a good account of itself in the Levant Crisis of 1840–41, despite the anxiety of inferior numbers to the French fleet that might support the Egyptians. A problem unique to the British admiralty was the need to create a naval force that matched the country's global needs in terms of different types of ships, as well as overseas bases.

The latter became more important with the development of steam-powered ships that required coaling facilities around the world. In home waters the problem created by steam ships was security against sudden attack from across the channel by a fleet no longer dependent on favourable winds (as William the

11

Conqueror had been in 1066). The first of numerous invasion scares occurred in the 1840s, when the prospect of a 'steam bridge' ferrying 20,000 French troops across the narrow seas was mooted by the Prince de Joinville. Much of the panic reaction to such nightmare scenarios stemmed from the acknowledged slowness of Britain's mobilization system. In a major war, the admiralty was confident of being able to mobilize two warships for every one that France could put to sea, but against a surprise attack it was a different story.

The outcome of the admiralty's numerous experiments with steam ships was that paddle steamers, however satisfactory for commercial purposes, were inferior to screw propelled warships. The problems of iron hulls remained unresolved. The solution, screw-assisted wooden sailing warships, restored Britain's naval supremacy and security by the 1850s to give her 'a position of unmatched global preeminence' in Kennedy's view, but it was an expensive one and only short term (**30**, p. 32). Confusion and uncertainty about the design of large ships persisted through the 1860s, creating 'a miscellany of ironclads' rather than a homogeneous battlefleet, but the decline of other navies gave Britain an easy lead in the 1870s. This complacency was suddenly ended in 1884–5 by a Franco-Russian challenge, creating fears that warships with 'Sardine box ends' – lacking armour plating front and rear – were floating targets for the technically superior French navy. This resulted in a major shipbuilding programme to restore Britain's supremacy at sea.

Despite the rise in the naval estimates to about £10 million by 1870, Britain was still spending an absurdly low amount of her wealth on defence – about 14 shillings and ninepence per head of the population. The army was, as always, the poor relation, in terms of public esteem that is. Large armies were associated with despotism. The army of 200,000 men in 1815 was soon halved in size and dispersed to the colonies and India. Hence Palmerston's acknowledgement in 1836 that 'England alone cannot carry her points on the continent.' A 'field force' of 20,000 men was about all that was available for service in Europe, prompting Bismarck's jokes about using Prussian policemen to arrest the British army in the 1860s. In the previous decade, an 80,000 strong militia had been raised to calm fears arising from yet another French invasion scare. The failure of the high command to organize the war effort in the

Crimea effectively destroyed the reputation of the British army. By 1885, however, it had regained not only its Waterloo strength but also some of its prestige, through successful colonial campaigns.

Political factors

In a parliamentary regime there may be a natural tendency to display less party political differences in matters of foreign policy than in contentious domestic issues. A bi-partisan approach seems to be the norm, therefore, unless a major issue of principle or security or morality arises. For most of the nineteenth century it is hard to discern a distinctively Liberal or Conservative foreign policy. What can be seen, however, is a display of differing attitudes to diplomatic problems and to relations with other states by Liberals and Conservatives. That said, it is hard to avoid the conclusion that the main influence on Britain's foreign policy at any given time was the temperament of the foreign secretary and/or the prime minister of the day. Indeed, British 'insignificance' in Europe in the late 1860s has been partially attributed to 'the personality and character of her foreign secretaries' (16, p. 226).

After the 1830 revolution in Paris, Palmerston spoke of the 'Principles and Policy of England and France' being 'pitted against those of the Absolute Powers'. But Canning, Wellington, and Peel (all Tories) agreed that an understanding with France was important to the peace of Europe. On the other hand, in 1858–9, the Conservatives (when temporarily in office) sympathized with the Austrians, while the Whig/Liberals supported the cause of Italian liberties. In 1863–4, the Conservatives once again supported the German powers (mainly Prussia) when the Liberal government had come out in favour of the Danes. On both occasions, the queen had made her pro-German feelings quite clear. With regard to Russia, it is obvious that the Conservative/Peelite Lord Aberdeen put remarkable trust in Tsar Nicholas, while Palmerston was inordinately suspicious of Russian aims in both the Near East and Central Asia. Palmerston was also critical of Aberdeen's conciliatory policy to the USA in 1842, attacking it as a 'humiliation' and a 'sacrifice of real interests and established rights'.

The differences in the views held by Aberdeen and Palmerston

13

cannot easily be attributed to their party differences. What is striking is the contrast in their temperament. Aberdeen had a conciliatory disposition to the point of 'wimpishness'. Palmerston was abrupt and abrasive in his zealous defence of British interests, as he saw them. Castlereagh and Canning were both Tories, even if the latter laid claim to some 'liberal' pretensions, but their attitude towards the European Concert was very much at variance.

In the Gladstone–Disraeli era, fundamental policy differences are readily discernible. Disraeli's pro-Turk stance at the expense of the Bulgarians provoked Gladstone's wrath in the famous pamphlet on the 'Bulgarian Horrors'. Gladstonian Liberals tended to see Russia as the Protector of the Balkan Slavs and were also pro-French. In the 1880s, by contrast, the Conservatives regarded the Triple Alliance (of Germany, Austria–Hungary, and Italy) as a bulwark against France and Russia. Furthermore, Disraeli succeeded, perhaps by accident, in making the empire a political issue, from which the Conservative party derived considerable electoral benefit, despite the initial setbacks in Afghanistan and South Africa. Ironically, it was the anti-imperialist Gladstone who took Britain into Egypt. His reluctance, however, was not shared by all his cabinet, so there is a genuine problem in determining how typical his views were of the Liberal party as a whole. His 'successor', Lord Rosebery, was certainly much closer to Salisbury's views on many issues, while the latter's predecessor, Lord Derby, might well have felt more at home in Gladstone's government than in Disraeli's, as actually happened in 1882.

Not that Gladstone's views on foreign affairs should be identified with the deeply pacifist, non-interventionist, approach of the Manchester School associated with Cobden and Bright. Gladstone insisted that for a country like England it was impossible that 'the affairs of foreign nations can ever be indifferent'. What marked Gladstone out from the rest was his internationalism, combined with a dangerous belief in morality in international politics. Not surprisingly, Bismarck could not stomach Gladstone, but he got on well with Disraeli.

Instead of a Liberal foreign policy and a Conservative foreign policy, the nineteenth century as a whole seems to exhibit two traditions. The internationalist, pro-European strand links Castlereagh through Aberdeen to Gladstone. Disraeli, on the other hand has often been seen as wearing the mantle of Palmerston, who was himself a 'Canningite', vigorously asserting Britain's interests. The distinction between the two traditions is sometimes made in terms of a 'passive' or 'active' policy, or between a 'consolidationist' or 'forward' policy

Foreign policy was largely determined by the foreign secretary and prime minister, usually with the advice of two or three senior ministers, supplemented on occasion by that of the service chiefs, but in a crisis or when a binding commitment was under consideration, the full cabinet would participate in determining policy. Few ministers had the time or inclination to wade through all the despatches on a regular basis. Hence Salisbury's objection to having to adapt foreign policy to the views of ministers who were 'usually ignorant of it and seldom united in their view'. Furthermore the whole cabinet was too big for effective decision-making. Not that this deterred Gladstone from holding interminable discussions, prompting the remark that 'nothing was ever settled satisfactorily in the cabinet' (14, pp. 16–17). What the cabinet could do was to lay down the general principles on which British policy should be based, such as whether or not to work in step with the Concert, or whether to act in conjunction with France in Iberian affairs. Similarly, the cabinet could decide if the independence of Belgium was to be encouraged in principle, while leaving the foreign secretary to work out how it could be achieved in practice. Parliament played an even more peripheral role, unless an alliance was being proposed. Debates on foreign affairs were not uncommon, but their influence on policy making was slight, even if ministers learned to be careful about the use of military force and the risk of heavy expenditures to achieve their objectives. This meant that the foreign secretary and the officials of the foreign office could enjoy a fair measure of autonomy in formulating policy. Their aristocratic backgrounds encouraged a sense of aloofness in the practice of the noble art of diplomacy as well as a disdain for vulgar interests, pressure groups, and the press.

The role of the press increased in importance by mid-century as newspaper circulation increased, following advances in print technology and faster rail distribution. Newpapers and periodicals provided full coverage of political events, including reports of parliamentary debates. Although politicians such as Palmerston or Disraeli tried to influence one or two editors who were well-disposed towards them, the press was very resistant to government pressure, embarrassingly so at times. Ministers often had great difficulty in persuading foreign diplomats that the views expressed in the leading newspapers were not inspired by the government. In its vigorous defence of national interests the press may also have harmed Britain's relations with Europe by its frequent disparagement of 'foreigners' – a case of nothing new under the *Sun*?

The Gladstone–Disraeli duel received much prominence in the press, whose overwhelmingly Liberal sympathies (at both national and regional level) were only beginning to wane in the 1870s. The growth of the press alongside the enlargement of the electorate arguably made 'public opinion' a force to be reckoned with. Hence Salisbury's concern that while 'Power has passed from the hands of statesmen', the fact was that 'the humour of our people is quite unpredictable'. He also complained in the 1890s that 'The diplomacy of nations is now conducted quite as much in the letters of special correspondents as in the despatches of the Foreign Office.' But whereas the press could probably influence government policy on certain issues, by its very nature it rarely, if ever, spoke with one voice and was not really capable of determining British foreign policy.

The influence of the monarch over foreign policy declined throughout the century. George III had played an important role in both domestic politics and foreign affairs until his health gave way. His son was much cleverer, but indolent. His obstinacy was sometimes a serious hindrance, as in the case of South America. His brother, William IV, was industrious and outspoken, but against a united cabinet he made little headway. Victoria, his niece, suffered a double disadvantage. The 1832 Reform Bill reduced the influence of the crown in the House of Commons, to which ministers were now more answerable and Victoria's youthful inexperience left her dependent on their advice in her early years. Nevertheless, ministers had a constitutional duty to consult the queen on foreign affairs, which gave her some leverage to convert legitimate influence into improper interference in policy-making. Victoria and Albert made an effective duo, until his death in 1861, while the queen's family connections, extending across Europe, provided her with a unique network of information. She was not discreet about her personal feelings. She came to distrust Palmerston and disliked Gladstone intensely, but fell for Disraeli's sychophantic flattery. Furthermore, by 1885 she had reigned for nearly half a century and had few inhibitions about making her views known to the prime minister or foreign secretary of the day, so she was quite capable of playing a central part in the decision-making process.

2

Castlereagh and Canning, 1815–27

Britain's role in the peacemaking process (1814–15)

Britain was able to exercise a great deal of influence over the peacemaking process in 1814–15 because she had played a major role, both diplomatically and militarily, in the final stages of the war against Napoleon. The Duke of Wellington's victories in Spain made him a military hero even before the battle of Waterloo in June 1815, while Viscount Castlereagh, Britain's foreign secretary since 1812, succeeded in consolidating the rather shaky alliance against France in the Treaty of Chaumont in March 1814.

As late as 1813 the anti-French coalition was still riven with discord and disagreements. The idea of making a separate peace with Napoleon continued to hold much attraction for the Austrian foreign minister, Metternich, while the Russians and Prussians were in collusion over the future of Poland and north Germany. The allied victory at Leipzig in October 1813 tended to aggravate the problem of discordant aims.

Castlereagh's mission to the continent in January 1814 to coordinate the policies of the allies was a brilliant success. His insistence that the great powers act together and create a general European settlement, not a series of *ad hoc* agreements as problems arose, was gradually accepted by the other powers. Castlereagh's determination was rewarded by the Treaty of

Chaumont, which envisaged a twenty year alliance to keep France in check, financed by a British subsidy. Britain was therefore able to exert decisive influence on the terms of peace offered to France after Napoleon's defeat and capitulation in late March 1814.

Although Britain was concerned about the European settlement in general, the top priority was understandably the peace treaty with France. Britain had not declared war on France in 1793 for ideological reasons but because of the invasion of the Austrian Netherlands (Belgium) and the threat of a French attack on Holland. Hence the insertion into this treaty of the scheme to unite 'Belgium' with Holland, so as to ensure that Antwerp and the Scheldt estuary, with their proximity to Britain's coastline, would be in safe hands.

Having secured a major strategic interest, Castlereagh could afford to adopt a more disinterested approach than the other peacemakers and play a leading role in the peace process. Since most of the powers had entered into prior commitments while the war was being waged, the peace negotiations were necessarily complicated by these earlier treaties.

The British attitude to France was remarkably lenient, even after Napoleon's escape from Elba and the battle of Waterloo. Her frontiers were fair, the Bourbons were restored to the throne and a constitutional charter provided basic political rights. Demands by Prussia and some other states for the dismemberment of France were firmly rejected. Castlereagh insisted that the recipe for a peaceful France was a mixture of generosity and firmness. Precautions were therefore taken against a resurgence of French expansionism by creating 'buffer' states or 'watchdogs' on her borders, with one of the great powers acting as a back up. The object was to deny French armies the easy passage they had enjoyed in the 1790s when they had overrun neighbouring states with remarkable rapidity. The union of the former Austrian Netherlands with Holland strengthened the barrier to the north, reinforced by the consolidation of various Rhenish duchies under Prussian rule. Similarly, the absorption of Genoa into Piedmont, reinforced by Austrian rule over Lombardy and Venetia, blocked the coastal route for French armies into Italy. In addition, the victors renewed their alliance against France for a further twenty years.

The vigorous defence of British maritime interests was only

to be expected when Britannia ruled the waves. The discussion of grievances arising from Britain's right of search (for contraband of war etc) during the war years was kept to a minimum, while the strategic control of trade routes, especially in the Mediterranean and around Africa, was consolidated. This underlined the fact that before the French war forced her to give priority to continental politics and her own security, Britain's main interests had been extra European and commercial. Retention of key conquests such as Malta and the Cape and some West Indian islands was axiomatic, but many other colonial conquests were returned to the Dutch, the Spanish and even the French, a generous act which puzzled Napoleon. The British also desired to secure a general condemnation of the slave trade.

The settlement of central Europe, largely dealt with at the Congress of Vienna, which met from September 1814 to the summer of 1815, was probably the least satisfactory part of the peace settlement from Britain's point of view. Castlereagh had hoped to see the creation of a strong central Europe, whose stability would be ensured by Austria and Prussia, acting as a barrier to Russian, as well as French, expansion. The success of his scheme depended on Austro-Prussian resistance to the aggrandizement of Russia, especially the tsar's claim to the whole of Poland. But as compensation for their likely territorial losses in the east, the Prussians demanded the whole of Saxony, whose king had been too hesitant in his desertion of Napoleon.

The 'balance of power' in Germany, and in Europe as a whole, depended on securing a reasonable solution to this Polish–Saxon crisis. When Castlereagh's initial strategy of aligning the two German powers against Russia broke down in December 1814, a compromise was sought. The new Poland would be reduced in size and Austria would agree to Prussia acquiring two-fifths of Saxony. Even so, it took a threat of war to secure Prussia's compliance with these terms. This crisis facilitated the creation of a weak federation of German states under Austrian influence, much to Castlereagh's disappointment.

The Italian settlement was also largely Metternich's work. Strategic considerations could be used to justify the dominant role of Austria in north Italy. The extension of her influence over the central duchies, however, as well as Rome and also Naples, was less desirable. Metternich had such a deep-seated hostility to constitutions that the chance was missed to give the Italian states the benefits of good government. Castlereagh was too much of a Tory to press the issue, arguing against too many constitutional experiments on top of those in France, Spain and Holland.

Castlereagh unquestionably played a major role in the peace-making process in 1814–15. If the Vienna settlement is regarded as a pragmatic and sensible response to the enormous problems that existed after the long wars, the British foreign secretary is entitled to a large share of the credit (**2B**, **36**). His reputation, however, suffered unjustly from the obloquy meted out by nineteenth-century liberals and historians, who greatly exaggerated the strength of nationalist feeling among the peoples of Europe in 1815 (**2B**, p. 33). A century after his death, however, a British foreign secretary paid tribute to his work, saying in 1926: 'as in the days of Castlereagh, Great Britain stands forth again as the moderator and peacemaker of the new Europe'.

Castlereagh and the 'Congress System' (1818–22)

Castlereagh is regarded as the most European-minded British minister before Edward Heath because of his desire for co-operation with the other powers and his belief in the European Alliance. Not that his contemporaries fully shared his enthusiasm for what Webster (**17**) has called (with some exaggeration) 'a new system of European diplomacy'. His cabinet colleagues were well aware of the basic insularity of British opinion after the long, exhausting war and of the public's natural preoccupation with the economic distress, that followed its ending. A further complication was the confusion in the public mind between the Alliance, linked to the treaty of Chaumont of 1814, and Tsar Alexander's 'Holy Alliance', conceived in 1815. Although the tsar's scheme was received with amused scepticism by Metternich and others, it was viewed with great suspicion by British opinion.

In his quest for a formula for a peaceful and stable international order, Castlereagh was not typical of British foreign secretaries in the nineteenth century. But to be bracketed with noted 'internationalists' such as Aberdeen and Gladstone is a dubious compliment – given that one premier drifted into the Crimean war in 1854, while the other left General Gordon to his fate at Khartoum in 1885.

For Castlereagh the basis for cooperation among the great powers was provided by Article VI of the Second Treaty of Paris of November 1815, in which the signatories agreed to 'renew their meetings at fixed periods . . . for the purpose of consulting upon their common interests' and to contemplate 'the measures which shall be considered the most salutary for the repose and prosperity of Nations . . .'. Obviously, Castlereagh's own experience of the successful negotiations in 1814–15, when he was in close personal contact with Metternich, Alexander, and Hardenberg and others, greatly influenced his outlook after 1815.

The series of meetings that were held between 1818 and 1822, known as the 'Congress System', was only one aspect of a complex diplomatic situation. The key underlying issue in the post-war period was the rivalry between Britain and Russia for influence in Europe (2C). Russia's grievance that Britain emerged supreme in 1815 led to ideas of an alignment or understanding with France, herself aggrieved at her limited freedom of movement after Vienna. This, in turn, encouraged cooperation between Britain and Austria in European affairs.

At the congress of Aix la Chapelle in 1818, summoned to deal with problems relating to France, signs of this tension and rivalry emerged. Strong support from Metternich, seconded by Prussia, ensured that Castlereagh's views that the congress should concentrate on the French issue and be restricted to the great powers prevailed. The importance of this success was underlined when the tsar put forward a proposal for an *Alliance Solidaire*, open to all states, guaranteeing existing thrones and governments. Such a far-reaching scheme went way beyond the Congress's terms of reference and, with Wellington's assistance, Castlereagh was able to persuade the tsar to abandon it.

The main business relating to France caused little dissension. Also, the problem of integrating France into the great power system was solved quite neatly by Castlereagh's suggestion that France be invited to join the discussions of the powers under Article VI of the Treaty of Paris of 1815. Other issues that were discussed but not resolved included the Spanish colonies and Russian intrigues at Madrid.

The second congress which met at Troppau in October 1820, was summoned in response to the political discontent that became widespread in the smaller states in the years 1819–20.

This unrest had a significant effect on the alignments of the great powers. It gravely weakened the Austro-British front because of the divergence of views publicly expressed by Metternich and Castlereagh towards the unrest, at least in Italy. At the same time, it made a Franco-Russian alignment much less attainable, partly because the tsar began to have second thoughts about flirting with liberalism, while the French bungled the opportunities presented to them by the revolt in Naples.

The political challenges that arose in Europe in 1819–20 called for considerable dexterity, at which Metternich excelled, because of the fluidity of the situations themselves and the uncertainties of the responses of the powers. Whereas Alexander was sympathetic to a 'sentimental and unreal Liberalism', Metternich condemned outright all expressions of discontent which Castlereagh, as a minister of a parliamentary regime, could not, even though he disapproved of 'this mania for constitutions'. A further complication arose from the alleged intrigues of Russian diplomats or agents in Italy and in the German states.

The murder of a Russian agent, Kotzebue, in March 1819 gave Metternich an opportunity to press a series of repressive measures, the Carlsbad Decrees, on the German states, aided by Prussia's servile attitude. Castlereagh's despatch of congratulations to Metternich is not surprising since he was in favour of similar measures in Britain – the notorious Six Acts of 1819.

In 1820, revolts against incompetent rulers broke out in both Spain and Portugal, but the liberal factions seemed unable to establish stable regimes, especially in Spain where the adoption of the 1812 constitution hampered good government. The British government saw no reason for the great powers to intervene in the internal affairs of states who were unlikely to 'infect' the rest of Europe with their liberal ideas or radical antics. The French, however, saw a chance to play a bigger role in international affairs if they persuaded the Spaniards to adopt a moderate constitution on the lines of the French 'Charter' of 1814. Prussia, on the other hand, prompted by Russia, demanded action against the new regime in Spain. Metternich, perhaps surprisingly, accepted Castlereagh's arguments formulated in a state paper in May 1820 that 'the Alliance was made against France', and was not intended for 'the Superintendence of the Internal Affairs of other States'. For the time being outside intervention in Spain was avoided, while British claims to exclusive influence in Portuguese affairs were reluctantly acknowledged by the other powers.

If the Alliance withstood the strains of unrest in Iberia and Germany, why did revolts in Italy result in a breach between Britain and the three Eastern Courts? One obvious reason could be that the Neapolitan revolt which broke out in July 1820 exacerbated an already tense situation, when the purpose of the Alliance was being called into question. The key factor, however, seems to have been that Metternich believed it was essential to secure a European mandate for Austrian intervention in Naples, a point which Castlereagh could not concede.

The problem of dealing with the Neapolitan revolt was made worse by the rebels' adoption of a constitution which made a reasonable compromise with the king impossible. This was a bad setback for French diplomacy in Italy, whose aim was to act as the patron of Bourbon constitutional rule, thereby creating an alternative focus of loyalty to Habsburg Austria. As for Russia, it was anybody's guess whether the tsar would opt for the constitutional cause or insist on the suppression of the revolt. Russia's support for the French demand for a congress was the only success France had. Cooperation with Russia proved more difficult than expected, partly because the French decision to follow the British example of sending 'observers' (not delegations) to the congress resulted in their being 'sidelined' and unable to exert much influence over the proceedings.

The basic question to be decided was whether Austrian troops should suppress the revolt or whether the Neapolitans should be persuaded to adopt a moderate constitution, acceptable to their king. The latter was the aim of both the Russian foreign minister, Capodistrias, and the French; Metternich demanded military action in the name of the Alliance; the tsar wavered; Britain refused to assent to a mandate. Castlereagh had no objections to the use of force by the Austrians, who had treaty rights with Naples. The problem was the mandate that Metternich insisted on for fear of a Russian countermove in north Italy once the Austrian army marched south. Metternich skilfully played on the tsar's fears of revolution, aided by news of a mutiny at St Petersburg, and secured his agreement to the Troppau Protocol, which gave Austria the blessings of the other two signatories in suppressing the revolt in Naples.

The Protocol, issued in November 1820, asserted that intervention in the name of the Alliance was justified when revolutions occurred endangering other states. Much to Metternich's chagrin, Castlereagh repudiated the notion that the Alliance justified the great powers in acting as the 'armed guardians of all thrones' and refused to allow Britain to be associated with 'the moral responsibility of administering a general European police'.

The Congress that reconvened at Laibach did nothing to heal the breach between Britain and the 'Holy Alliance' powers. Its avowed aim was to mediate between King Ferdinand of Naples and his people, but in reality the main purpose from Metternich's point of view was to secure the acceptance of the delegates from the Italian states of the decisions made by the congress, without much discussion of the issues.

The Neapolitan revolt was duly suppressed by Austrian troops in March 1821, with the blessing of the tsar, who reacted to the news of a rising in Piedmont by offering 100,000 men to put it down and by warning France against intervention. By the spring of 1821, Metternich had good reason to be satisfied with his handling of the Congress. Almost the whole of Italy was now under Austrian military surveillance. Tsar Alexander had virtually abandoned any support for Liberalism and France had failed to play the Bourbon card over Naples effectively. The only drawbacks were Castlereagh's open rejection of the Troppau Protocol and Alexander's insistence that it be applied to Spain. News of an outbreak of revolt in Greece naturally caused some alarm until Metternich persuaded the tsar that it was the work of a revolutionary conspiracy centred on Paris, and not a noble cause that Russia should support.

At the Congress of Verona, which met from October to December 1822, the main subject of discussion was not Greece, but Spain. On both of these issues, however, Britain and Austria had similar views, so it was possible for Castlereagh and Metternich to try to restore their earlier cooperation in European affairs.

The Greek revolt against Turkish rule, which broke out in April 1821, was initially a failure. It became much more successful when the Morea became the main centre of revolt. After initial indifference, public opinion in Britain and France swung round to an active agitation in favour of the Greeks, mistakenly

25

regarded as descendants of the Heroes of Antiquity. In Russia, widespread pro-Greek sentiment, encouraged by the Orthodox Church, reinforced existing grievances against the Turkish government over the non-fulfilment of the Treaty of Bucharest of 1812.

Russia's demands for the backing of the Alliance for intervention against the Turks had no chance of success. Castlereagh regarded the Russian claim to act as protector of the Greeks as little more than a cover for expansionist designs in the Near East. At a meeting with Metternich at Hanover in October 1821 Castlereagh discussed various tactics to restrain Russia from precipitate action. A four-point plan was devised to meet her concern over the fate of the Greeks, together with a commitment to diplomatic activity at Constantinople to persuade the Turks to meet Russia's other grievances. Since both France and Prussia agreed to give their backing to the Hanover programme, the Alliance was clearly denying Russia a mandate to intervene. Eventually, patient diplomacy at Constantinople secured enough concessions to enable Metternich to persuade the tsar to await the meeting of another congress in the autumn of 1822, at which Alexander intended to raise the issue of Spain.

Before 1820, the 'Spanish problem' meant the problem of the colonies in Latin America which had been asserting their independence of Madrid from 1812 onwards. Both Russia and France pressed for military aid to Spain to enable the king to suppress this colonial revolt, but Britain objected strongly, partly because her trading links with South America had greatly increased during the Napoleonic wars. To avoid encouraging republicanism, Castlereagh favoured the idea of setting up independent monarchies in the colonies.

The outbreak of revolution in Spain itself in January 1820 complicated the issue of the colonies. Castlereagh saw that recognition by Britain of the independence of the colonies would damage the prestige of the new government in Madrid. But when it failed to make any headway in the negotiations with the colonists at a time when the United States seemed increasingly likely to accord recognition, Castlereagh decided that Britain should act by granting commercial recognition to them. He also hoped to persuade the allies at the Congress of Verona to concede diplomatic recognition to the colonies.

In Spain itself the political situation deteriorated in 1821–2, so that by January 1822 complete anarchy was said to prevail. Castlereagh feared that a Franco-Russian front was likely over Spain, while the tsar was demanding the despatch of a European army to Spain. This problem was going to be a major issue at the Congress of Verona, but before it met Castlereagh had committed suicide, in August 1822, as a result of stress and overwork.

In a sense, the Congress System died with Castlereagh. His successor disliked congresses and without Britain, one of the leading powers of the age, any other sort of meeting hardly counted as a congress. It became obvious that the Congress System was born of special circumstances – the experience of close personal contact in the final stages of the war against Napoleon – something that could not be prolonged for ever (2C). Even Castlereagh's great prestige could not prevent the emergence of serious strains in the alliance, as shown at Troppau, though his presence at Verona might have made a lot of difference to the outcome, since he and Metternich were largely in agreement over leaving Spain to her own devices. As a form of 'summit diplomacy' the Congress System was an interesting experiment, but it lacked structural underpinning or organization. The collapse of the Congress System did not mean the demise of the Concert of Europe – it simply necessitated finding an alternative, and possibly more flexible, forum for great power diplomacy. Such an alternative already lay to hand in the form of conferences of ambassadors. In fact, given the confusion that the leading statesmen of the time displayed over the terminology of their diplomatic assemblies, it may well be that the term 'The Congress System' is largely an invention of history examination boards.

Canning: France and 'Spain with the Indies' (1822–27)

Canning's previous experience as foreign secretary made him the obvious successor to Castlereagh whose views on Spain, Portugal, and Greece were broadly similar. George Canning was also a highly talented politician whose parliamentary skills were much needed by Lord Liverpool's government for the arduous and important role of leader of the House of Commons.

Although Canning and Castlereagh had much in common as regards the substance of their policies (the major exception

27

being their attitude towards the Congress System) they were strikingly different in terms of the presentation of their views. One of Castlereagh's shortcomings was his aloofness. He was a poor communicator. He was both clever and industrious and good at constructing an argument, but his delivery was very laboured. This shows even in his written despatches, such as the State Paper of May 1820, which yields very few quotable extracts despite its length and gravitas.

By contrast, one of Canning's greatest gifts was the art of communication. He was a superb showman whose misfortune was to have been born before the age of the mass media. In his policy towards Latin America, for example, he is said to have 'converted a routine operation into a splendid publicity campaign' (**22**, p. 260). In a famous speech made in 1826, some years after the event, he declaimed with great fervour that 'if France had Spain, it should not be Spain "with the Indies". I called the New World into existence, to redress the balance of the Old.' A splendid piece of 'bombast', this has been called, echoing the view of a contemporary critic that his speeches contain 'better sounding phrases than solid sense'. Nevertheless, there is no doubt that Canning's neat turn of phrase (the equivalent of the modern 'sound bite'?) and oratorical skills won support for his policies in the House of Commons. They also made a strong impact on the press and public opinion in the country, as well as impressing liberals abroad (**23, 35**).

Not that Canning's success can be ascribed solely to his ability to present his policies in terms which his audience would readily understand and approve. His views were soundly based on a mastery of detail and he possessed a breadth of vision and a quickness of intellect equalled by few of his rivals or successors. He is commonly regarded as an outstandingly successful foreign secretary (**22, 23**).

Yet, as a recent critic of Canning's Greek policy has observed, 'few British statesmen have enjoyed as charmed an afterlife, among both their contemporaries and their scholarly admirers, as has George Canning' (**34**). Castlereagh's ghost might justly be aggrieved that Canning, contriving always to be 'on the side of the angels', became the hero while he was cast unfairly as the villain of British foreign policy. In fact, Canning's reputation as a liberal both at home and abroad was a bit bogus, and derived from his well-publicized dislike of the Holy Alliance, his marked hostility to Metternich, and his moderate sympathy for smaller states' aspirations for freedom (22).

Still, Canning's policies towards Portugal, South America, and Greece count as successes. British prestige was enhanced and British interests were well defended, without exposing the country to great risks. War was avoided, expenditure was modest, and Britain's liberal image was enhanced – not a bad formula for a popular foreign policy. All this was achieved despite considerable political difficulties. Until 1825 he had to contend with the personal animosity of the king, George IV, who intrigued with foreign diplomats behind his back and encouraged cabinet colleagues to oppose his views. Canning had little or no personal following in the Commons – his supporters numbering no more than about twenty – while the High Tories were very suspicious of him and his policies as became evident in 1827, when the premiership fell vacant. The Duke of Buckingham told the king that 'the Tory Party detest Mr Canning', insisting that 'Mr Canning will not do. Everyone is proud of his talents, but no one trusts his principles.'

One of the issues on which Canning and the king disagreed was Europe. Proud of his knowledge of continental politics, the king was a strong believer in the Concert of Europe, whereas Canning, who lacked Castlereagh's personal experience of 'summit diplomacy', advocated disengagement from the continent. Hence his rejection of Castlereagh's strategy of attempting to weaken the neo-Holy Alliance with French aid, while keeping the Congress System going. Canning favoured simply destroying the Holy Alliance regardless of the effect on the Congress System.

Canning's decision not to attend the Congress of Verona in person, as Castlereagh had intended to do, but to send the Duke of Wellington as Britain's representative was symptomatic of his attitude. Castlereagh had hoped to use his influence with the tsar to divert Alexander from pressing for action over Greece and Spain, while restoring good relations with Metternich after the disagreements over the Congresses of Troppau–Laibach. He also hoped to persuade them of the need for recognition of the independence of the Spanish colonies. Canning had no chance of success on such issues at Verona.

By the time the congress assembled at Verona, Greece had ceased to be the most pressing issue for the great powers.

Russia's other grievances against Turkey had been met and the tsar had been persuaded that the revolt in Greece was a 'rash and criminal enterprise'. This put the affairs of Spain at the top of the bill. Wellington rejected the French plan for intervention in Spain to restore the king's powers. The French retaliated by refusing to agree to the idea of British mediation between France and the Spanish government (the 'rebels'). Both states then joined with Austria in vetoing the Russian suggestion of sending an allied army to Spain. But, with the Spanish king appealing to his fellow sovereigns for aid and some plan needed to satisfy the tsar who had relented over support for the Greeks, Metternich had to come up with a gesture of some sort, to avoid the worst-case scenario of a Russian army marching across Europe. Hence the rather bizarre solution of simultaneous protest notes to the regime at Madrid by four of the great powers in the hope that its response might justify more effective action against the revolution.

The failure of the Congress of Verona to resolve the problem of Spain meant that France would feel free to act in support of the king without a European mandate and at a time of her own choosing. Canning seems to have misread the situation, believing that unilateral action by the French was unlikely, even though the new foreign minister, Chateaubriand, was known to be pressing for military intervention.

The French invasion of Spain in early April 1823 was a serious setback for Canning, who found it difficult to satisfy his liberal critics. The best he could manage was to secure three assurances from France: that the military occupation would not be permanent; that Portugal would not be attacked; and that Spain's overseas colonies were not under threat. In return for these concessions, Britain agreed to remain neutral. Not that she had much option. Canning's contemptuous attitude towards the European alliance ruled out any possibility of an appeal to the other powers for collective pressure on France. Canning was therefore forced to stand by helplessly while French troops overran Spain and restored Ferdinand VII's full powers. When the French army reached Cadiz in September 1823 without meeting serious resistance, contrary to Wellington's predictions, Britain's humiliation was complete (2D, p. 64). The fate of the Spanish colonies also seemed to hang in the balance.

The importance Canning attached to Latin America was

underlined by his statement in November 1822 that 'no questions relating to Continental Europe can be more . . . vitally important to Britain than those which relate to America.' In a sense, of course, such views are more a reflection of the new foreign secretary's priorities (if not prejudices) than a profound assessment of Britain's interests in this period. Canning regarded recognition of the independence of the Spanish colonies by Britain as a major issue, but before 1823 he wanted to avoid a clash with the government at Madrid over it. Like Castlereagh, he hoped for the creation of monarchical regimes, rather than republics, in Latin America partly perhaps to lessen the hostility of the king and the High Tories in the cabinet to his policy. Naturally, Canning felt there was a bonus to being first to accord recognition, if only to score over the United States, with whom Britain's relations were not very cordial.

The most pressing aspect of the issue in late 1822, however, was commercial. British merchant ships were being attacked by so-called pirates, with the connivance of the Spanish authorities in Cuba and elsewhere, or even confiscated by them for trading with rebels. With over eighty commercial houses active in South America, Britain's economic stake was much more substantial than her rivals'. If the government at Madrid was unable or unwilling to act to protect this trade, one alternative was to seek the cooperation of the colonial authorities in the ports of the region, which implied recognition of their political status. But, to avoid a major clash with Spain, Canning resorted to despatching an extra naval squadron to the West Indies in October 1822.

The French invasion of Spain in April 1823 changed the situation completely. It was no longer a question of good relations with the government at Madrid but of deterring a French reconquest of the Spanish colonies in the name of the king, especially after the occupation of Cadiz in September 1823. An attempt at an understanding with the United States in August made no progress. The Americans insisted on prior recognition of the colonies by Britain as the price of their participation in a public declaration to warn off the French. Much more successful was Canning's direct approach to France in October 1823. The French ambassador, Count Polignac, was persuaded to put on record in an official memorandum assurances that his government had no ambitions to appropriate any part of Spain's colonies or to seek exclusive advantages. This disclaimer proved to be a valuable diplomatic weapon the following spring.

The announcement of the Monroe Declaration by the president of the United States in December 1823 complicated the situation for Canning. In publicly opposing European claims to influence and territory in the Americas, the United States seemed to be intent on placing itself at the head of an American Confederacy, directed against Europe. In fact, the declaration was aimed in part at Russia who had recently restated exclusive claims to territory and trade in Alaska and the North West. Since it was Britain's sea power that dominated the Atlantic, Monroe's pretensions seemed somewhat inflated, but they also reinforced Canning's aim of deterring any attempt at a reconquest of Spain's colonies.

The American connection was also useful as a means of resisting French pressure on Britain to attend a congress of the European powers to solve the problem of the Spanish colonies. In a sense, the French had boxed themselves in over Spain and Latin America. They wanted to prevent Britain from securing advantages in trade and influence and hoped to place Spanish Bourbon princes on the thrones of the South American states. What they could not do, however, as Spain's ally, was to accord recognition to the colonies. They hoped to resolve the dilemma through a congress, but Canning outwitted the French by refusing to attend the congress unless the United States was invited. He also published the Polignac Memorandum, thus ruling out any idea of French troops being used to assist in a colonial reconquest.

The question of recognition by Britain remained. In 1824, commercial interests and public opinion were pressing for it and relations with America would be eased by taking this step. The problem was the king, supported by Wellington and the High Tories. When Madrid persisted in refusing to negotiate with the colonists, Canning decided to press ahead with the policy of recognition. By December the cabinet had been won over, partly through fear of the French connection but also because of Canning's threat to resign. Before the end of the year Buenos Aires, Columbia and Mexico had been recognised by Britain as *de facto* independent states. The loud remonstrances from the other European states made Canning's policy seem like a major diplomatic triumph. In reality some of the colonies had been effectively independent for at least a decade and, in any case, Canning had inherited the policy from Castlereagh. No risks were involved, thanks to Britain's sea power. The main opponent Canning faced was the King of England, backed by some of the cabinet.

By cultivating relations with the new states, Canning, exploited the colonists' goodwill to the advantage of British trade and influence. But for several decades trade and investment did not expand as much as had been anticipated. The economic benefits, in terms of trade and investment, came after 1850, especially from 1865 to 1913. Still, Canning had the satisfaction of having checked the influence of the United States in South America – not a bad reprisal for the Monroe Doctrine?

When Canning needed an arena to demonstrate British influence in Europe, especially as a counter to the French success in Spain, Portugal was the obvious choice. Although Canning's assertion in 1825 that 'Portugal has been and always must be English' was a typical overstatement, it could reasonably be claimed that a 'special relationship' existed between the two states, thanks to the Methuen Treaty of 1703 and the fact that British troops had defended Portugal from Napoleon's armies. The long coastline and the accessibility of Lisbon from the river Tagus made Portugal very open to the influence of a naval power. In the 1820s Portugal also had a supposedly 'constitutional' regime, but Canning had a pretty low opinion of the government of 'rascally, thieving, ragamuffins' at Lisbon (**22, 23**).

The danger that Portugal might become a satellite of a French-dominated Spain, obliged Canning to respond to its request for a territorial guarantee, even though his main aim was to restrain the Portuguese from rash actions that would embroil Britain. His reluctance to become involved in Portuguese affairs was soon justified by events.

The return of King John to Lisbon in 1821, after an extended 'exile' in sunny Brazil solved one problem but created another. It ended the rule of the corrupt regency which had provoked an army revolt in 1820 but led to a revolution in Brazil, where his elder son, Dom Pedro, was proclaimed emperor. Worse was to follow. His younger son, Dom Miguel, plotted against his father in Portugal, so that King John became a virtual prisoner for a time after a coup in May 1823.

Portuguese politics became very confused and complicated. Absolutists, such as Miguel and the queen (a sister of the king of Spain) aided and abetted by the French ambassador, plotted against the legal government, winning support from some of the army. Constitutionalists, who were mostly loyal to King John, looked to Britain for support. The question facing Canning (and later foreign secretaries) was whether British interests in the region justified becoming involved in the appalling tangle of Iberian politics.

In 1823 it was decided to reject the request for troops, but to send a naval squadron to the Tagus as a sign of British concern. The fleet also provided a 'safe haven' for the king when the Miguelites became a serious threat. In the following year it was the French ambassador's turn to become chief plotter, even changing sides to try to win the king's favour, and attempting to bring French troops across the border from Spain. Canning, reluctant to commit British troops to Portugal, countered by threatening to despatch Hanoverian forces to Lisbon as a warning to the French government, which agreed to disavow the intrigues and antics of its ambassador.

Canning explained his adoption of a more 'forward' policy on three grounds. Firstly, that the presence of French troops in Spain was seen as a symbol of defeat for British influence in Iberia. Secondly, (and not very convincingly) that Portugal was the chosen ground for a confrontation between the Continental Alliance and Britain, requiring a riposte for the sake of British prestige. More serious was the argument that a settlement between Lisbon and Brazil was being hampered by the advice given by foreign diplomats (especially the French ambassador) to use force against the 'rebels'. Clearly, if a hostile expedition were to be prepared in the Tagus, the position of the British fleet would become untenable. A settlement of the dispute with Brazil, on the other hand, preserving a monarchical regime at Rio, could facilitate recognition of Spain's American colonies by reducing the hostility of the Tory cabinet to such a policy.

British attempts at mediating between Lisbon and Rio were initially unsuccessful. Both father and son were under pressure from their advisers to take a tough line in the negotiations. But Canning persisted, anxious to bring about a settlement, and secured the dismissal of the French ambassador whose influence

34

was too strong for Canning's mediation to succeed. Eventually, in August 1825, the mission of Sir Charles Stuart to Lisbon and Rio brought about an agreement on the terms of Brazil's independence.

Less than a year later, the death of King John caused a renewal of tension and strife in Portugal. Partly a dispute over the succession, the crisis also revived the old battle between absolutists and constitutionalists. Dom Pedro, the elder son, renounced his claim to the throne in favour of his eight-year-old daughter, Donna Maria, with his sister to act as regent. This arrangement displeased Dom Miguel, even though he was expected to marry the young Maria in due course. The most controversial feature of Dom Pedro's plan, however, was to endow Portugal with a new constitution, to replace the one abrogated during the unrest in 1824.

Dom Miguel's displeasure was widely shared – with the ultras, the king of Spain, and Metternich – to name but a few. Even Canning had his doubts whether it would add to the country's stability. Spain's action in arming deserters from the Portuguese army threatened the new regime at Lisbon until Canning's visit to Paris in September 1826 put a stop to the French ambassador's support for the Miguelite deserters at Madrid. A renewed threat in November was checked by British protests to the Spanish government but when a major incursion into Portugal began in December, Canning decided to respond to Portuguese requests for military support by sending 5,000 British troops to Lisbon 'to plant the standard of England on the heights of Lisbon' so that 'foreign dominion shall not come', as he rather dramatically put it.

Britain's intervention had some effect. The troops were warmly received in Lisbon and they put new heart into the Portuguese army's resistance to the Miguelites, who were abandoned even by the Spanish king. Plots and dissensions nevertheless continued to complicate Portugal's political life, but Canning was able to secure an agreement with France in April 1827 for the withdrawal of their respective forces from Spain and Portugal. The principle of non-intervention was thereby respected – until the next Iberian crisis required British and/or French intervention, which happened on five occasions between 1815 and 1848 (**2D**, p. 59).

British policy and the Greek revolt (1821–31)

Britain's main interests in the Greek revolt were the maintenance of peace and the preservation of British influence at
Constantinople, objectives that were not necessarily all that
compatible. Canning, being Canning, would also regard satisfying public opinion as a desirable aim, unlike Castlereagh, or
later Wellington, who objected that 'there never was such a
humbug as the Greek affair'.

By 1825, after the intervention of Egyptian forces had turned
the tide against the rebels, the revolt presented Britain with a
dilemma. Inaction would either result in defeat for the Greeks or
lead to a Russo-Turkish war that could extend way beyond the
confines of Greece. Action, on the other hand, meant siding with
Russia in an anti-Turkish policy and at the least, applying strong
diplomatic pressure on the sultan – a potentially useful ally.

Most accounts of British policy in the Greek revolt give
Canning the benefit of the doubt, interpreting his change of
front in 1826 as a sign of flexibility and assuming that his death
just before a major crisis arose in 1827 exculpates him from the
confusion that followed. A recent critic, however, has suggested
that if Canning was really playing a 'waiting game' then he
ought to have had a clearer idea of what it was he was waiting
for (34). According to this interpretation, Canning had no
policy to solve the Greek revolt, displaying almost complete
indifference to the problem until mid-1825. His negative attitude towards the Russian plan for a conference at St Petersburg,
combined with his suspicion of France and his contempt for
Metternich may well have left him little room for manoeuvre.

Canning's view of Russia was much the same as that of
Castlereagh – suspecting her of expansionist designs in the Near
East and of looking for an excuse to intervene in the revolt in
order to realize them. His view of the Greeks was totally devoid
of sentiment or ideological sympathy, regarding their leaders as
'a most rascally set', which put them on a par with Portuguese
reformers.

In this he was being much more realistic than the philhellene
organisations which shared Shelley's simplistic view that 'We
are all Greeks', reflecting the dominance of classical studies in
a gentleman's education. What public opinion did not really
appreciate was that 'Greek' was at this time a religious rather

than an ethnic label. For example, in the Morea, the main area of the revolt, Turks and Greeks were similar peoples but with different religious beliefs. Not that this inhibited the Greeks from massacring 20,000 Morean Turks. Since 'Greeks' were scattered all over the Turkish empire, as merchants or administrators, the Greek revolt would have made more sense, perhaps, as a sort of 'takeover bid' for running the Turkish empire (**24**, p. 198).

In recognizing the Greeks as belligerents in May 1823 – a move condemned by the other powers – Canning was simply protecting British commerce from 'piracy', but he insisted on total neutrality by Britain. Russia's role in the Greek revolt was complicated by her disputes with Turkey over other issues, which led to the breaking off of diplomatic relations in August 1822. If it was in Britain's interest to try to bring about a restoration of diplomatic relations between Russia and the Sublime Porte (the sultan's regime) it was not to Canning's liking to play the role of mediator on Russia's behalf, however much he wanted to see a solution of her grievances. If mediation was needed, it was between Turkey and the Greeks, who made an appeal to Britain for aid in October 1825 in another attempt to secure their independence from the sultan.

Canning's refusal to participate in a congress on the Greek problem in January 1824 to discuss the Russian plan for the creation of three autonomous provinces was badly received by the other powers. The rejection of the plan in October by both Greeks and Turks, however, let Canning off the hook. Russia's frustration was increased in early 1825 when France and Austria refused the backing of the Alliance for a war against Turkey, despite the desperate plight of the Greeks after the intervention of the Egyptian forces under Ibrahim Pasha.

The way to break the deadlock was for Canning to see the need to begin a dialogue with St Petersburg in order to avoid a Russo-Turkish war. Since Alexander wanted a *rapprochement* with Britain (having failed to persuade Metternich of the need for action to defend the Greeks against the rumoured Egyptian threat to depopulate the Morea by 'ethnic cleansing') an agreement seemed both possible and desirable. Even then it took until April 1826 to conclude the Anglo-Russian Protocol, which envisaged autonomy for the Greeks to be achieved (hopefully) by the mediation of the two powers. The delay was partly due to the death of Alexander in December 1825, but also to the British government's reluctance to allow Russia a free hand against Turkey if mediation failed.

Canning's persuasion of the French to adhere to the modified protocol after his successful visit to Paris in September 1826 was a clever move. The French king was keen to respond to the philhellene mood of public opinion, while his ministers were concerned with France's commercial interests in the Near East and also feared Russian expansion. In addition, the signing of the Convention of Akkerman in late 1826, settling disputed issues between Russia and Turkey, reduced the risk of becoming involved in war.

The Treaty of London of July 1827, to which Austria and Prussia refused to accede, was nevertheless full of danger. A secret article talked of interposing between the belligerents (if an armistice were rejected) to prevent 'all collision' between them, 'without however participating in the hostilities' – an anticipation, seemingly, of UN/NATO decisions in Bosnia in the 1990s. Worse still was the threat of 'ulterior measures' to be taken if the crisis remained unresolved, with instructions to the admirals of the allied fleets couched in similarly vague terms.

If Canning accepted the need to threaten the use of force, the cabinet, as well as Wellington, were far from happy with it. The Greeks, however, were in great danger of defeat by 1827 and Tsar Nicholas was on the rampage, threatening unilateral action. Canning's refusal to work through the Congress System meant that he was unable to check Russia by drawing in the two other conservative powers. Although British cooperation with Russia and France split the European Alliance, much to Canning's satisfaction, it forfeited Austria's restraining influence over Russia.

The risks involved were revealed after Canning's death in August 1827. When the Turks rejected the armistice proposed in the Treaty of London, the allies resorted to blockading the Egyptian forces in the Morea. Admiral Codrington's orders did not cover the eventuality of being fired on by hostile forces, so he solved the problem by sinking the Turco-Egyptian fleet at Navarino in October 1827.

Wellington called it an 'untoward event' and a policy of drift ensued. The Turks became more intransigent and began a holy war against Russia in April 1828. French troops were sent to the Morea, while Russian armies made great strides in 1829 and reached Adrianople, threatening the Turkish capital. By the Treaty of Adrianople, Russia made valuable gains in Asia Minor but made only modest demands in the Balkans. Russian expansion was not held in check by Britain, nor by the defunct Holy Alliance, but by her own restraint.

Negotiations dragged on from 1829 to 1831 in London to settle the Greek issue, especially its frontiers and its status. Aberdeen, the new foreign secretary, sought compromises with the French and the Russians, but Wellington, the prime minister after Canning's death, was obstinate even after Russia's victories. Eventually, the powers agreed on an independent Greek kingdom with modest frontiers but the final terms, including the identity of the new ruler, were not agreed until 1831, by which time Palmerston had become the new foreign secretary.

Britain and the European balance of power (1815–30)

The changes in the European balance in this period were mostly related to the ending of the war. Hence France recovered her status as a major power, especially after the successful invasion of Spain in 1823. As a military power, this placed her second to Russia, whose unduly large peace time army cast a shadow over the continent. Britain, on the other hand, ceased to be a serious military power once its war time army was disbanded. Her naval power was maintained and influenced the fate of the Spanish colonies and Greece. Austria, meanwhile, extended her influence over Italy and Germany, but debatably at the cost of over-extending herself.

Changes in the relationships among the great powers were mainly the result of the rash of revolutions in the smaller states. The Anglo-Austrian entente was gravely weakened and the chance of a Franco-Russian alignment was lost. It also created a division between the Eastern Courts, who accepted the Troppau Protocol, and the western powers. The split was not final, as the alignment over the Greek revolt showed, when Russia collaborated with France and Britain. Canning may have killed the Congress System, but the Concert of Europe was able to survive in a more flexible form, as demonstrated by Palmerston's use of conference diplomacy after 1830.

3

The Palmerstonian age, 1830–65

Palmerston: Foreign Secretary and Prime Minister (1830–65)

From his appointment as foreign secretary in 1830 until his death in 1865, Palmerston's main political interest lay in foreign affairs. His interest in domestic issues was limited, although he was a great believer in the importance of social union as the basis of true patriotism. Britain's moral authority abroad, he asserted, depended on the 'good behaviour of all . . . classes' and the stability that resulted from it (**3A**).

His first spell at the foreign office was as a member of the great Whig reform ministries of Lords Grey and Melbourne (1830–41). Unlike Canning, Palmerston was something of a 'late developer', holding only 'hack' jobs until his mid-forties, so he was lucky to be offered the foreign office in 1830. He was foreign secretary again (1846–51) under the 'arch whig of the nineteenth century', Lord John Russell, who became premier after Peel split the Tory party over the repeal of the Corn Laws. Palmerston's impetuous recognition of the new regime of Louis Napoleon in December 1851 led to his dismissal, when the impatience of his colleagues was in harmony with the annoyance of the queen.

Palmerston's energy and widespread popularity made him the obvious successor to the ineffective Lord Aberdeen as prime minister in February 1855 to provide more vigorous direction to the war against Russia. With first Clarendon, an accomplished if timid diplomat, and then Russell, a notorious 'busybody' and self publicist, at the foreign office for most of the next ten years (1858–9 excepted), Palmerston continued not only to determine the substance of foreign policy but also to explain this policy to the country. His relationship to public opinion was interactive, in that he allowed himself to be influenced by it but also appealed to it when he was in difficulties. He described public opinion as one of 'the two powers in this country' (together with government) which had to be in agreement on major policy issues.

Palmerston came to be greatly admired by the press and public opinion, but foreign diplomats objected to his outspoken comments and abrasiveness, which earned him the title of 'Lord Pumicestone'. From being an indifferent speaker in public and in the House of Commons, Palmerston suddenly discovered in 1847 an affinity with a large audience which gave him the confidence thereafter to speak impromptu in parliament and at public meetings, thereby boosting his popularity.

His 'John Bull' image seems easy enough to understand, yet there was something elusive about him. Some of the unresolved contradictions in his policies and personality might stem from being 'a compound of Castlereagh and Canning'. But perhaps it was simply that being an opportunist, a man of expedients, there were bound to be inconsistencies in his attitudes especially over a time span of 35 years. After all, Canning, whose foreign policy supposedly had overall coherence, held office for only about five years. The great Lord Salisbury, a future foreign minister, condemned Palmerston for displaying 'all bounce and baseness' in his conduct of Britain's foreign policy, while Disraeli accused him, probably unjustly, of 'pseudo-liberalism', but his critics cannot deny his charisma and popularity as 'the Most English Minister' (**3A**, **38**).

Palmerston personified the self-confidence of the middle classes of mid-Victorian England. The period from 1850 to 1870 was one of unparalleled prosperity, which Englishmen attributed to economic freedom, personal liberty and a free press. Palmerston himself believed that the virtues of a constitutional system of government were self-evident. Foreign diplomats, who curiously failed to see it, mistakenly regarded him as a Radical, intent on fomenting disorder on the continent. Equally mistaken was the view of British liberals that Palmerston was the champion of nationalism in Europe. His real objective, according to Steele, was to draw attention to Britain as an example of a modern state that worked, where stability and prosperity were the benefits to be derived from constitutional monarchy allied to free enterprise capitalism (3A, p. 63).

The defence and furtherance of British interests were naturally regarded as the basic aims of British foreign policy. If peace with the European great powers and the USA was the top priority, keeping an open door for trade was also a task he took seriously. This responsibility might necessitate 'police actions' to punish foreign regimes for obstructing trade or for financial default, but these were unlikely to be frequent since, Palmerston asserted, 'An example now and then tends to keep the rest in order.' A fundamental concern was the security of the British Isles especially in the 1850s when the transition from wooden to iron ships or ironclads put Britain's naval supremacy at serious risk, leading to renewed invasion scares. If his conviction in 1857 that 'No powerful nation can ever expect to be really loved or liked by any other' was made with half an eye on France, he nevertheless felt that constitutional states were 'the natural Allies of this country'. But given his stark belief that 'the interests and views of nations perpetually clash' (3A, p. 28), Palmerston took the line that Britain had no eternal friends and no eternal enemies, as his attitude to France and Russia in 1840 shows.

Belgian independence and crises in the Near East (1830-41)

In the Belgian crisis of 1830–39, Palmerston probably acted under the close surveillance of the prime minister, Lord Grey, until 1834 (21). The later of the two crises involving the sultan and Mehemet Ali in 1839–41, represented one of Palmerston's most constructive achievements. These two issues, involving relations with both France and Russia, the two key players in international affairs in the 1830s from Britain's point of view, illustrate the value of flexibility in diplomacy.

Ambivalence towards France and suspicion of Russia seem to

characterise much of the Palmerstonian period. When France became a more parliamentary regime after the 1830 revolution, it made possible a greater degree of cooperation between her and Britain as defenders of the cause of constitutionalism in Europe against the autocratic regimes of the three Eastern Courts. But Palmerston also suspected the French of expansionist designs and attempted to set limits to the growth of their political influence in Europe. Similar suspicions were held of Russia in the 1830s and 1840s and Palmerston wrongly attributed expansionist policies to her in the Near East. Nevertheless, he seized the opportunity to cooperate with Russia in defence of the Ottoman Empire in 1839–41, even at the risk of a possible war with France. The dilemma which Palmerston failed to resolve was that Britain needed France if she was to cut a figure in Europe, since she could not play a major role on the continent without a large army. Palmerston's mistrust of France, however, ruled out a serious alliance (**3A**, p. 60).

By November 1830, when Palmerston took over the foreign office, an ambassadorial conference was already in session in London trying to find a peaceful solution to the crisis created by the Belgian revolt. A provisional government at Brussels had earlier proclaimed the independence of Belgium from Holland. This was not strictly a 'nationalist' revolution, since the political boundaries in the former Netherlands were not based on linguistic or religious divisions, but it was a major challenge to the Vienna settlement and a threat to peace.

Clashes between the Belgians and Dutch troops were not the only danger. Conflict among the great powers was a distinct if shortlived possibility. Russia was ready to join Prussia in objecting to this attack on the 1815 treaty, while Austria would make common cause with them in defence of monarchical rights. The new regime in France, on the other hand, could hardly tolerate the suppression of a popular movement whose inspiration owed much to events in Paris, and was under pressure to act boldly by those who favoured the annexation of Belgium to France.

Securing assent to the principle of 'non-intervention' was therefore a major success of the conference in the early stages of the crisis. The Anglo-French accord on Belgian independence also acted as a serious discouragement to military intervention by Russia and Prussia. This became even less likely after a rising in Warsaw in late November. The problem of French ambitions remained. Opportunities for France to secure favours in return for supporting the Belgians were difficult for the government at Paris to pass up. Territorial gains; partition between France and Holland; a French prince on the Belgian throne – all these temptations arose and threatened a major clash with Britain. By mid-January 1831, however, such tensions were greatly eased when the conference agreed to a self-denying clause for all the great powers.

War might also arise from a clash between Holland and Belgium. Although the king of Holland had accepted the principle of Belgian independence in January 1831, the 'bases of separation' provided numerous opportunities for disagreement. Financial questions were complex and technical and boundaries were disputed, especially the Belgian claim to Luxembourg. The establishment of a monarchy was another highly charged issue especially when the Belgians' first choice fell on a French prince, the duc de Nemours, and they had to be persuaded to accept Leopold of Saxe-Coburg, a more neutral candidate, instead. Terms which were acceptable to the Dutch were rejected by the Belgians, and vice versa, so that Palmerston was engaged in negotiating a series of compromises through the spring of 1831, but to no avail. Hostilities broke out in August. Coercion of the Dutch who had occupied Antwerp, required a French army and a British naval squadron, but the sympathies of the three Eastern Courts lay with the king of Holland. When the French troops proved reluctant to leave Belgium, Palmerston, with the backing of Prussia and the other powers, threatened France with war.

Agreement on the terms of independence for Belgium was reached in November 1831 but even then King William's acceptance of the Convention was withheld until June 1833. The Dutch eventually yielded to further coercion by Anglo-French forces, despite the unease of the other powers. The agreement on Belgium's neutrality had to wait until 1839.

Resolving the crisis without a war was a major achievement for which Palmerston was entitled to much of the credit. He worked very hard as chairman of the conference of diplomats representing the five great powers, showing great resource in finding forms of compromise that could provide the terms for a settlement that at times neither side seemed to want. Above all, perhaps, Palmerston demonstrated a way of exploiting the tensions among the great powers in a constructive fashion – a fine example of adroit diplomacy (**18**).

Palmerston held a more optimistic view of the Ottoman Empire's chances of survival than did many of his contemporaries. Hence his alarm at the threat to the sultan's regime when Mehemet Ali, pasha of Egypt, who was aggrieved at the meagre rewards for his aid during the Greek revolt, went to war against his suzerain. Syria and Palestine fell to his son, Ibrahim, in 1831. By December 1832 he had defeated the Turkish army sent against him and was advancing on Constantinople.

Although Palmerston regarded this as 'a crisis of the utmost importance to all Europe', the British cabinet was singularly unmoved (**21**). Emerging from the Reform Bill crisis, and averse to an open ended commitment when scarce naval resources were fully occupied along the Belgian coast, the government turned down the sultan's appeal for aid. This 'tremendous blunder', as Palmerston called it, was a heaven-sent opportunity for the Russians, whose warships and troops were invited to defend the Turkish capital. Their reward was the Treaty of Unkiar Skelessi of July 1833, in which the sultan agreed to close the Dardanelles to all foreign warships if Russia were attacked by another power.

Palmerston was unduly suspicious of this treaty and held a very exaggerated view of the advantages Russia secured by it. He was also mistaken in assuming a connection at this time between Russian activities in the Near East and Central Asia, but it contributed to his determination to undo the 1833 treaty.

The opportunity presented itself in 1839, when the ageing Sultan Mahmud decided on a war of revenge to recover Syria from his vassal. It was a total disaster. His forces were routed and his fleet deserted to the Egyptians. At his death, the fate of the Ottoman Empire was in the hands of a boy of sixteen and Constantinople once more lay open to invasion. But this time the great powers were seemingly ready to come to the rescue. A Collective Note in July 1839 assured the sultan that they had decided to find an agreed solution to the crisis.

The consensus among the powers was shortlived. France put pressure on the sultan to make more concessions to Mehemet Ali, thereby delaying the negotiations, to the advantage of her protégé. Palmerston would have no truck with this ruse. He was convinced that Ali's occupation of Syria was a threat to British interests in terms of trade routes to the Persian Gulf, which Ali had reached in 1838, and to the Red Sea route to India, to defend which Britain had taken Aden in early 1839.

Since the Russians also regarded Ali as a menace, an anti-Egyptian front seemed possible, despite the temptation for them to exploit the rift between Britain and France. Russia's shaky finances also prompted a *rapprochement* with Britain, whose firm policy in Central Asia had impressed the tsar, as did the strength of the Mediterranean Fleet. In late 1839, Russia offered to cooperate against Ali and not to seek renewal of Unkiar Skelessi, in return for Britain's agreement in principle to the closure of the Straits. This was very acceptable to Palmerston, but not to the cabinet, (most of whom were either russophobes or francophiles) until the French premier, Thiers, overplayed his hand in March 1840. This enabled Palmerston to secure an agreement among the other four powers, excluding France, on how to resolve the crisis (11, p. 257).

In the Treaty of London of July 1840, the four powers accepted the principle of the closure of the Straits and agreed to offer Ali hereditary rule of Egypt with possession of Syria for his lifetime. A strict deadline for acceptance of these terms was imposed. The reaction in Paris was very hostile but Palmerston was confident (even if the cabinet were not) that French indignation would not mean war.

Fate smiled on Palmerston. The military action went remarkably well. In September, Beirut was bombarded by British warships and Turkish troops were landed successfully. Acre fell two months later after a lucky shot hit the magazine store. By February, Ibrahim's forces had withdrawn to Egypt, the Turkish fleet returned to base and Ali acknowledged that hereditary rule over Egypt alone was his best bet.

Although France was invited to join the other powers in signing the Straits Convention of 1841 and the Egyptian settlement, Palmerston had ignored the opportunity for a *rapprochement* with France when the more pacific Guizot replaced Thiers in November 1840. This sort of snub was hardly statesmanlike. On the other hand, Palmerston's critics tend to underplay the extent to which his tough attitude towards France earlier in the crisis was justified by Thiers' defiant and deceitful attitude (13). It was not unreasonable to fear that a possible outcome of the crisis could have been a French protectorate over Egypt, in line with their occupation of Algeria in 1830, and a Russian ascendancy over Constantinople, leaving Britain with nothing unless she was prepared to fight. Palmerston's policy at least had the merit of limited military action and the preservation of the Concert of Europe through cooperation with Russia.

Britain and the European balance (1830-48)

The 1830 revolution in France was hailed by Palmerston as an event 'decisive of the ascendancy of Liberal principles throughout Europe'. But in September 1833, Metternich succeeded in persuading the tsar to reaffirm the principle of conservative solidarity at their meeting at Münchengrätz, effectively reviving the Holy Alliance of 1815. A few months earlier Britain and France had failed to cooperate in the Near East, allowing Russia to pull off at least a prestige gain in the Treaty of Unkiar Skelessi. In 1847, Metternich was to assert that: 'Abandoned by France and defeated on every diplomatic field, England now finds herself alone and paralysed in the face of the continental powers' (**13**, p. 61). Hardly a testimony to Palmerston's diplomatic achievements, even allowing for his being out of office from 1841 to 1846, but Metternich was not known for generosity towards opponents.

Palmerston devoted a lot of time and energy to events in Spain and Portugal, especially in the 1830s. Why Britain should want to become involved in the tangle of Iberian politics is not easy to understand. Canning, of course, had made great play of it, but interference in the internal affairs of other states was supposed to be contrary to Liberal principles. Palmerston admitted as much in 1847 when he said that intervention in Portugal was a 'very unusual measure for the British government to take' and that it was more typical of Russia and Austria. Nor was the logic very clear that justified Anglo-French intervention but denied the the conservative powers the same right (**2D**, p. 78).

One attraction of Iberia was that it constituted an appropriate area to demonstrate the vitality of the Liberal Alliance which, in turn, might help to deter Russia from pursuing expansionist ambitions. The formation of the Quadruple Alliance in 1834 with France, Spain, and Portugal enabled Palmerston to boast of having created a 'powerful counterpoise to the Holy Alliance'. But Palmerston did not intend France to gain much from the arrangement. In Portugal, Britain was to intervene alone, but in

Spain the two great powers would act together, if not in harmony. Sending token forces of warships, marines or 'volunteers' to support the Constitutionalist cause, in association with France, was also a relatively cheap way of pleasing public opinion. The complex mixture of dynastic claims and ideological conflicts could be neatly simplified for public consumption, with the Absolutists, (Carlos and Miguel) cast as the 'wicked uncles' of the young queens (Isabella and Maria).

A Spanish army and a British naval force achieved a quick success against Miguel in May 1834, but Carlos was made of sterner stuff. The good work of an Anglo-French naval force and British volunteers was nullified by the farce of Carlos' escape from 'captivity' in England. The civil war in Spain consequently dragged on until 1839.

The Quadruple Alliance could hardly be said to have been a brilliant success. Britain's influence on the outcome was limited, but Palmerston took comfort from the fact that unilateral action by France (as in 1823) had been prevented. On the other hand, Britain found herself obliged to intervene again in Portugal to blockade a rebel base at Oporto in 1847, but this time the rebels were Constitutionalists, protesting against Queen Maria's dictatorial regime.

The Liberal Alliance fell apart in 1846 because of the tension between Britain and France over the affair of the Spanish marriages. Palmerston was much to blame, being his usual forthright self when a more tactful approach was called for. This was an issue that was not worth souring relations with France over. It seems doubtful whether Palmerston correctly evaluated the effect on British interests of a French prince eventually becoming king of Spain (13).

A supposedly amicable agreement had been reached in 1845 between Guizot and Lord Aberdeen, that both the Orleanist and the Coburg candidates (the latter a relative of Queen Victoria) were precluded from marrying Queen Isabella. Aberdeen may have conceded, however, that Montpensier (a younger son of the French king) could marry the queen's sister, the Infanta, once the queen had produced an heir. It followed that the only permissible suitors for Isabella were her cousins, the Spanish Bourbon princes, Don Francis and his younger brother Don Henry, neither of whom had much to recommend them. To add spice to the endless gossip, it was rumoured that Don Francis was impotent but in reality it was probably Isabella who had an infertility problem.

By the time Palmerston was back in office in July 1846, the regent was plotting with the British ambassador to marry off her daughter Isabella to the Coburg prince, whose morals and politics were preferable to those of Don Francis. When Palmerston blundered in, sending a despatch that ruled out the French prince but not the so-called 'English candidate', Guizot claimed complete freedom of action to arrange a double marriage to include Montpensier and the Infanta. This revelation of French 'treachery' tended to overshadow Palmerston's own misdemeanours.

The decline of the Liberal Alliance was further evident in 1846, when the free city of Cracow was occupied by Austrian troops, and Palmerston rejected a French proposal for a joint protest against the violation of the 1815 treaty. In Switzerland the French even sided with Metternich in the interests of the *Sonderbund*, the Catholic cantons, who opposed the attempt by the twelve Protestant cantons to revise the powers of the Federal government in favour of greater liberalisation. The French hoped to take the lead in concerted action by the great powers to restore order and maintain the 1815 system. Palmerston, however, responded to the Protestants' appeal for aid by resorting to delaying tactics. This enabled them to win a military success before an international conference was summoned, so they duly secured reform of the Federal system in December 1847.

In Italy the election in 1846 of a Liberal Pope, Pius IX, caught Metternich totally unprepared. As a gesture to papal independence a British naval squadron arrived off the west coast of Italy, to warn France and Austria off intervention at Rome. More quixotic still was Palmerston's decision to send Lord Minto to Tuscany and other states to advise on timely constitutional reform, so as to avoid revolution. Not a successful mission, as 1848 shows.

Palmerston's response to the 1848 revolutions was very restrained. Since Britain and Russia were the only major states to be unaffected, it made sense for them to use their influence in the interests of peace among the great powers. Palmerston was seemingly willing enough to put his liberal sentiments aside for the sake of the balance of power. Hence his lack of sympathy for German unity, his concern for Austria as a great power, and his fear of France embarking on crusades for Italians and Poles.

To prevent the growth of French influence in north Italy, Palmerston proposed strengthening Piedmont as a buffer state, but he badly misjudged the military and political situation in north Italy. Anglo-French mediation on behalf of Piedmont in September 1848 made little progress. In the south, Palmerston's open support for the Sicilian rebels was also of little avail. By the summer of 1849, the *status quo ante* prevailed throughout Italy, but this was not a major concern for Britain.

His refusal to recognize Hungarian claims to independence was based on the belief that Austria's survival in central and eastern Europe was vital to the balance of power. Nevertheless, to counteract Austrian and Russian pressure on the sultan to hand over political refugees, he used diplomatic and naval intervention at Constantinople. Similarly, he was less than prompt in offering an apology to the ruthless General Haynau who was roughly handled on a visit to London in 1850.

Palmerston's first attempt to grapple with the Schleswig-Holstein problem was quite successful. Although Holstein and southern Schleswig were predominantly German in population, the two duchies were linked to Denmark by a personal union with the monarchy. The Danish attempt to use force to strengthen dynastic claims to the two duchies led to a revolt in April 1848. German national feeling at the Frankfurt parliament insisted on Prussian troops being sent to evict the Danish forces from Holstein, which was a member of the German Confederation. Following Russia's request for British diplomatic support against Prussia, Palmerston found himself on a tightrope, attempting to discourage the Prussians while not encouraging the Danes. The fighting continued on and off until July 1850. In May 1852, the dispute over the duchies was settled in favour of the Danish crown, not the German claimant, the Duke of Augustenberg.

Palmerston's attitude to the issues that arose out of the 1848 revolutions seems to confirm that he put preservation of peace and the balance of power above other considerations. Despite this, he increased his reputation at home not only as a patron of liberalism but also as a friend of Italian unity.

Palmerston's 'gunboat diplomacy' – China and Greece

'Wherever British subjects are placed in danger', Palmerston wrote in 1846, 'thither a British Ship of War ought to be . . . to remain as long as . . . may be required for the protection of British interests.' This definition of 'gunboat diplomacy' seems innocuous enough but moralists and idealists at the time denounced his rough and ready treatment of foreign susceptibilities. Public opinion, on the other hand, was overwhelmingly on Palmerston's side, responding to his appeal to jingoistic sentiment. Whether Victorian imperialism was more insensitive than modern China's treatment of Tibet is perhaps debatable.

The root of the problem in Anglo-Chinese relations was not the opium trade, but Palmerston's insistence that foreign states show respect for British nationals and the normal conditions of civilized commercial intercourse. However, Chinese officials, who could be no less arrogant than western merchants, were not easy to negotiate with. The display of serene confidence in their cultural superiority belied the fact that China's golden age was past and that what westerners came face to face with was incompetence and corruption. Furthermore, both governments had problems with the slowness of communications, which allowed local officials to adopt high-handed attitudes that might be difficult to disavow several weeks, if not months, later when the news reached London or Peking.

In 1839 a conflict began over the seizure of opium by Chinese officials at Canton. This was part of an attempt to stop opium imports from India, which had grown sevenfold in the previous twenty years, financing the export of tea. The action of the Chinese in placing the entire British trading community (including the consul) under a form of house arrest seemed unjustified to British officials in the region. In London, the punishment of smugglers and the ban on an illegal trade were felt to be reasonable enough, but the affront to the crown's representative and the arrest of innocent citizens seemed to require retaliatory action. The despatch of an expeditionary force from India was therefore endorsed. A clash between Chinese and British warships escalated into a naval war by June 1840. In 1841, a major battle took place in which Chinese war junks were sunk and shore batteries captured.

By the Treaty of Nanking in August 1842, the Chinese agreed

to an indemnity and to the opening of five ports (including Shanghai and Canton) to foreign trade, with a resident consul in each. Hong Kong island was also ceded outright, but full diplomatic recognition still proved elusive.

In the years before the second China War of 1857–60, British merchants were pressing for the further opening up of China. France, Russia and the USA were also showing a keen interest in China's potential for economic exploitation. The persistent refusal to grant diplomatic recognition also meant that Anglo-Chinese relations were at the mercy of events.

The *Arrow* affair was just such an incident, which an able diplomat at Peking could have settled quickly and amicably. News of the incident, which occurred in October 1856, did not reach London until February 1857, by which time local officials had adopted a hard line from which it was difficult to retreat without losing face. The British were mostly in the wrong (15, p. 36). A Chinese vessel, owned by a British national and registered in Hong Kong, was boarded by Chinese officials on suspicion of piracy, probably correctly. Twelve of the crew, who were Chinese, were arrested. The owner claimed immunity from Chinese jurisdiction, although it transpired that his licence was no longer valid and, contrary to first reports, the ship was not actually flying the British flag at the time. The British consul at Canton, a young man of limited experience, over-played his hand in demanding a written apology from the Chinese for the affront to British prestige. Worse still, the governor of Hong Kong, Bowring, gave his full backing to the consul and agreed to the bombardment of the residences of the Chinese officials at Canton.

What was the British government to do? Disavow its agents and risk a severe blow to British prestige? That was not Palmerston's way. 'If we permit the Chinese . . . to resume . . . their former tone of superiority', he said, 'we shall very soon be compelled to blows with them again.' Palmerston's belligerence in backing Bowring, however, was fiercely attacked in the House of Commons, where a motion of censure was carried against him. But Palmerston won a resounding electoral victory over his critics in a campaign defending British subjects and the British flag against insult from 'insolent barbarians'.

Fresh from his triumph, Palmerston decided to secure a revision of existing treaties with China but negotiations failed.

Participation in an expedition was offered by France, to avenge the murder of a French missionary. Russia and the USA also gave diplomatic backing. Military operations in December 1857 against Canton went well, leading to the treaty of Tientsin in June 1858. Diplomatic recognition was at last accorded to foreign powers and extra-territorial privileges were confirmed. Ten new treaty ports were agreed and the interior was opened up to foreigners, including missionaries. The opium trade was legalised, since suppression had proved to be beyond the powers of the Chinese government.

The second China war did not end with the treaty because the Chinese postponed ratification of it and proceeded to debar a high-ranking British official from access to Peking by force. To compound their error, the Chinese tortured or killed British and French officials captured after a force of 20,000 allied troops had taken the Taku forts. It was this atrocity by 'a half civilized government' that was avenged by the burning of the Summer Palace (their place of captivity) in Peking in October 1860.

In the Don Pacifico affair of 1850, Palmerston's gunboat diplomacy nearly resulted in a defeat in the House of Commons. The incident involved a shady character making inflated claims for compensation against the Greek authorities for damage done to his property in the course of an anti-semitic attack in Easter 1847. The victim was not an Englishman, but a Portuguese Jew who claimed British citizenship by virtue of being born in Gibraltar.

What induced Palmerston to get on his high horse in such an unpromising cause? The answer was partly the principle involved – that Don Pacifico had been denied redress when he was clearly entitled to some compensation. More compelling, perhaps, were the numerous existing grievances against the Greek government for affronts to British citizens and British interests. The misgovernment and corruption that abounded in Greece gave the British government much to complain about. The proximity of a British fleet to Athens in January 1850 provided the means to threaten a blockade if the Greek government proved obdurate.

Palmerston put himself in the wrong by ignoring the fact that Greece was under international protection, which obliged him to consult with France and Russia. The French insistence on mediation produced a compromise agreement in London. News of it, however, was slow to reach Greece where the blockade was reinstated on the initiative of the British minister, reflecting the petty jealousies and rivalries between the French and British legations. The French naturally complained loudly and recalled their ambassador from London (21).

Palmerston's critics had a field day. Defeated in the Lords, a further defeat seemed inevitable in the Commons. But Palmerston pulled out all the stops, appealing to the Britons' exaggerated sense of pride and patriotism with the boast that an Englishman in trouble abroad could be sure that 'the watchful eye and strong arm of England will protect him against injustice and wrong'. He won a triumph in the Commons and the country, but his cabinet colleagues and the Queen had had enough of his bravado and subsequently seized on the chance to secure his dismissal from office in December 1851.

Aberdeen and the origins of the Crimean War (1854–6)

Aberdeen's conciliatory disposition was unquestionably a useful asset for a prime minister in the confusing political situation that existed in Britain after the Tory party split in 1846. In December 1852, Peel's former foreign secretary was able to form a coalition government of 'Peelites' and Whigs, in which Clarendon soon took over the foreign office from Russell, the former Whig premier. Palmerston, disgraced for his premature recognition of Louis Napoleon a year earlier, had to be content with the home office. This was a talented government, with great potential for domestic reform, but with very divided views on foreign affairs, especially as regards Russian policy towards the Ottoman Empire. While Palmerston and Russell suspected Russia of harbouring designs on European Turkey, Aberdeen, seconded by Clarendon, had more faith in the tsar's good intentions and hated 'the detestable character of Turkish tyranny' over the Balkan Christians. Another weakness was that the premier lacked the authority to dictate to the cabinet, whose deliberations seemed endless. Hence the suggestion that a little more energy and vigour in Downing Street might have prevented the war (24).

If Aberdeen and Palmerston held the same initial premise – that the tsar did not want war – they diverged completely on how to react to it. Palmerston, whose firm line in Central Asia in 1839 had won the tsar's respect, was all for warning off the Russians by clear signs of Britain's intent to resist any encroachment on Turkey. Aberdeen, by contrast, who regarded the Turks, rather than the Russians, as 'barbarians', persisted with quiet diplomacy until he gave in to the 'hawks' in the cabinet in September and December 1853. As a result, British diplomacy was both hesitant and ambiguous for much of that year just when it needed to be clear and consistent.

If the war was an accident, as is widely believed, Lord Aberdeen was certainly culpable. A man of peace, who lacked Palmerston's 'manly vigour', his willingness to compromise may well have been interpreted as weakness. Palmerston's desire to resist any infringement of Turkish integrity was well known, but he was not in charge of policy-making. Obviously, he was a powerful figure in the cabinet with allies, such as Lord John Russell, but the 'wild men' were often out-voted. Palmerston has even been cast as the villain of the piece, alongside the ambassador Stratford de Redcliffe and the Turks, in a modern reappraisal by Norman Rich (**26**). His evidence, however, is neither new nor altogether convincing. It seems more reasonable to accept that it was the belief that Russia was out to dominate the Balkans that motivated Palmerston, who saw the issue in terms of the balance of power. The general consensus favours the argument that war might have been avoided if either Aberdeen's policy of conciliation or Palmerston's firmer approach had been followed consistently. It was the mixture of the two that proved disastrous.

A fundamental issue in 1853 was the trustworthiness of the Russians in their professions of respect for Turkey's integrity. Aberdeen and Clarendon were prepared to give the tsar the benefit of the doubt, believing that Russia only wanted to safeguard the ancient rights of the Orthodox Church in the Ottoman Empire. The main danger as they saw it was that the Turks would seek to embroil Britain in their quarrels with Russia. Others, however, including Palmerston and Russell, suspected that Russia was out to establish a virtual protectorate over the sultan's twelve million Orthodox Christian subjects, which would greatly increase her political influence in Turkey.

The mission of Prince Menshikov to Constantinople in the spring of 1853 raised this issue in an acute form. His arrogant and overbearing manner made him a poor choice to head a diplomatic offensive to reassert Russian influence after the recent successes of the French and the Austrians. The Convention which contained Menshikov's demands was seen by the British and French ambassadors as 'fatal to Turkey's independence' because of its possible political implications. Lord Stratford de Redcliffe, was too turcophile for Aberdeen's taste, even though he used his influence with the sultan to restrain the Turks at critical moments. Aberdeen was more likely to be impressed by the views of the Russian ambassador, Brunnow, who assured him in late May that 'we do not ask for new powers of interference, we state only the existing law' (**27**, p. 148).

Menshikov's mission was a failure, signified by his dramatic departure from Constantinople on 22 May. To put pressure on the Turks, the tsar threatened to occupy Moldavia and Wallachia (future Roumania) the Danubian principalities under the sultan's suzerainty.

The British government, under increasing pressure from public opinion and the press to resist Russia, was forced to consider fleet movements as a gesture of support for Turkey. Consensus was lacking on the fleet's destination, so in June 1853 it anchored at Besika Bay, outside the Dardanelles. Even so, Aberdeen lamented that 'we are drifting fast towards war'. Palmerston and Russell who feared that French support would be forfeited by delay, wanted to send the fleet into the Black Sea if the Russians carried out their threat to occupy Moldavia and Wallachia, which they did in early July.

Diplomacy came to the rescue in the summer of 1853 in the form of a conference of the non-involved powers, presided over by the Austrians. The outcome was the Vienna Note, a formula intended to preserve the sultan's independence while satisfying the tsar's honour. It was accepted by the tsar on 1 August, but rejected by the sultan on the 20th. The failure of the Vienna Note brought war much nearer. Who was to blame? Aberdeen, who was all for forcing the Turks to accept it or face Russia alone, was convinced that Stratford had failed to use his full influence with the sultan. This criticism is possibly unfair (**27**, p. 145; **13**, p. 75).

In September, Nesselrode, the Russian foreign minister expressed the view that Turkey was obliged 'to take account of Russia's active solicitude for her co-religionists'. This so-called 'violent interpretation' of the Vienna Note shattered all

Aberdeen's illusions about the tsar's aims (**24**, p. 484). No longer could he believe that Russia's policy was pacific and honest whereas Turkey was belligerent and unreliable. Palmerston's assertion that the tsar's object was simply to take Turkey 'by sap rather than by storm' seemed vindicated by Russia's double dealing. Clarendon, believing that war was now inevitable, agreed with Aberdeen to authorize the summoning of the fleet to Constantinople, where war fever was so high that the council declared war on Russia on 3 October.

Despite this, diplomacy seemed to have another chance. In fact, if the war itself could reasonably be called 'a series of negotiations punctuated by battles', the prelude to it might be regarded as a series of crises punctuated by negotiations. At a meeting at Olmütz in early October, the tsar assured the Austrian emperor that he only wanted to affirm Russia's existing rights, thereby repudiating Nesselrode's 'violent interpretation' of the Vienna Note. He also promised to evacuate the Principalities when a modified Note had been signed.

News of Olmütz and the Turkish declaration of war reached London on 7 October, when the cabinet was deep in discussion of the crisis. Russell's scheming to replace Aberdeen as prime minister was thwarted by the latter's decision not to resign after all. As a result, Aberdeen gave priority to holding the cabinet together, rather than following his own instinct that Olmütz provided a real chance for a peaceful solution to the crisis (**27**, p.192). Russell discounted Olmütz as yet another example of Russian deceit and insisted on action being taken for the sake of British honour. Palmerston urged that the fleet be sent into the Black Sea, but the peace party won the day. Diplomacy would have to move fast, however, because the Turkish army was preparing to cross the Danube.

A variety of diplomatic initiatives designed to provide the tsar with an honourable retreat, such as the Collective Note, were under consideration when the 'massacre' of Sinope took place. On 30 November 1853, a Turkish flotilla was sunk by Russian warships in the Black Sea, causing heavy loss of life. This was a legitimate act of war, but it made nonsense of the tsar's promise not to escalate the crisis while the diplomatic negotiations were continuing.

Sinope was a giant stride towards war. In both Britain and France the press and public opinion were incensed by the 'massacre', which the presence of the allied fleets in the Black Sea could have prevented, as Palmerston had urged. Even *The Times*, usually well-disposed towards Aberdeen, asserted that Russia had thrown down the gauntlet to the maritime powers. Palmerston insisted that British honour had been stained, but Aberdeen, disdaining the popular clamour, would consent to little more than belatedly moving the fleet into the Black Sea in January 1854, causing Russia much offence. As late as mid-February Aberdeen was still insisting that war was not inevitable, but positions had hardened so much that an allied declaration of war was eventually issued on 28 March.

After two years of indecisive battles but enormous suffering, peace was finally agreed in March 1856 on the basis of the Four Points of 1854. Their aim had been 'to seek means for connecting the existence of the Ottoman Empire with the general balance of power in Europe'. Although the British government had accepted them as early as July 1854, their interpretation caused problems later. Palmerston replaced Aberdeen as premier in January 1855, by which time the Russians agreed to the Four Points as a basis for negotiations, but neither diplomacy nor military activity made much progress until the end of the year. Even in 1856 Palmerston wanted to extend the scope of the war against Russia but few shared his enthusiasm for converting the conflict in the Crimea into a real 'Russian War' on a wider front (**37**).

From Britain's point of view the most important aspect of the Treaty of Paris was the neutralization of the Black Sea, which prohibited Russia from keeping warships and naval arsenals there. The Russians regarded this as an unacceptable humiliation for a great power to endure and were determined to reverse it as soon as possible. Russia therefore became a 'revisionist' power instead of being a defender of the *status quo*. Turkey's integrity and independence were placed under a European guarantee, reinforced by an additional treaty, and Russia's 'special relationship' with regard to the Balkan Christians was ended. Turkish promises of reform were not to be relied on, on past showing. The granting of autonomy to the Danubian provinces, soon to become independent Roumania, was designed to set up a buffer state between Austria and Russia, who forfeited part of southern Bessarabia to Moldavia. The Austrians were the main beneficiaries of the creation of a European

58

commission to regulate navigation on the Danube. It is not easy to reconcile these terms with the sacrifices made in the war, except for the fact (which Taylor emphasises) that 'The war shattered both the myth and the reality of Russian power' (**33**, p. 82). If Russia needed to be checked in the 1850s, this was achieved by 1856, despite the bungling of the military and naval operations.

Britain and the European balance (1856–65)

By the time of Palmerston's death Britain's influence on the continent was waning and it continued to weaken in the late 1860s. Whereas in 1856 Britain had emerged victorious from the Crimean War, by 1865 the decline of the Anglo-French alliance and the rise of a Russo-Prussian entente created a favourable diplomatic situation for Bismarck's military gambles.

In the cause of Italian nationhood, their common sympathy for liberal–nationalism enabled Britain and France to act creatively. They failed dramatically, however, in the case of Poland and Schleswig–Holstein. Palmerston was willing enough to cooperate with Napoleon III, despite his fear that Bonapartism could mean expansionism, and a brief but intense war scare in 1859. The foreign secretary, Lord John Russell, on the other hand, was much less inclined to give Napoleon the benefit of the doubt.

Napoleon's campaign to liberate North Italy from Austrian 'oppression' was already under way when Palmerston returned to office in June 1859 after a brief Conservative interlude. The 'war of liberation', however, stopped well short of its objectives. The bloody slaughter of Magenta and Solferino led to a premature truce at Villafranca, with Venetia still in Austrian hands and the central duchies (such as Tuscany) destined for return to Habsburg rule.

Palmerston was denied cabinet support for a treaty with France if Austria used force against the duchies because of the hostility of both the non-interventionists in the government and the queen. But diplomatic pressure succeeded in making possible the union of the duchies with Piedmont, after a genuine plebiscite (one of Napoleon's favourite 'democratic' devices). His acquisition of Savoy and Nice as his reward, however, was resented by public opinion in Britain, making future co-operation more difficult.

The fate of Naples and the Papal States was also decided by Britain and France. Garibaldi's plan to liberate Naples from Bourbon tyranny, after his triumph in Sicily, alarmed Napoleon, who proposed a joint naval blockade to keep him off the mainland, to which Palmerston seemed agreeable. Russell, however, won the argument that Britain stood to lose influence in Italy if the Neapolitans supported Garibaldi. His triumphant campaign in Naples was checked before he reached Rome, thanks to timely intervention by Piedmontese troops. Referenda, of a questionable nature, produced large majorities in the Papal States and Naples for union with North Italy. Russell's famous, if fanciful, despatch of 27 October 1860, in which he spoke of the 'gratifying prospect of a people building up the edifice of their liberties' gave Britain's blessing to the Kingdom of Italy, proclaimed in the following March.

The most striking feature of British policy towards Italy, Bourne suggests, was its anti-French nature, seeking to restrain France by cooperating with her (13, p.104). British diplomacy generally lagged behind events, but muddling through resulted in an outcome acceptable enough to the British government and public opinion, if not to the queen and some High Tories. The radical nationalist picture of Palmerston as the architect of Italian unity was, however, quite bogus since in his view what made Italian nationalism 'safe' was its 'Whiggish' nature, in that only about two per cent of the population were enfranchised.

The Polish revolt of 1863, a nationalist protest against Russian rule, revealed the limits of British power and influence and showed just how conservative Palmerston's view of Europe was. Popular indignation against Russia in both France and Britain pushed the two governments into making protests but their actions were not coordinated. French proposals for joint pressure at Berlin to deter Prussia from assisting Russia in suppressing the revolt made Palmerston suspect that Napoleon wanted an excuse to threaten the Rhenish provinces. Proposals for a joint protest to St Petersburg also failed, so Russia was able to brush aside British diplomatic protests. Palmerston and Russell took a realistic stance that military intervention would be 'hazardous and expensive beyond calculation' and made a dignified retreat from the failure to do anything to aid the Poles, but it was much less easy for France to do so.

In the Schleswig–Holstein crisis of 1863–4 the weakness of the Anglo-French alliance was even more obvious and without French military support naval operations in defence of Denmark would be fruitless. Despite this, Russell chose to assert that Britain 'could not see with indifference a military occupation of Holstein', while Palmerston warned the Germans that 'it would not be Denmark alone with which they would have to contend' (**19**, p. 307; **12**, p. 118).

The Danish king's attempt to incorporate Schleswig into Denmark in March 1863 sparked off loud protests in Holstein and in the German Diet. The 1852 treaty was in ruins but the British government had no clear idea what should be done. The occupation of Holstein by German troops in December 1863 was followed by an invasion of both duchies, and of Denmark itself, by an Austro-Prussian force in the following spring. The Danish appeal to Britain prompted Russell to devise a plan for Anglo-French mediation backed by force, but Palmerston vetoed military intervention. This might be seen as an example of Palmerston's 'realistic assessment of Britain's limited capacity to influence events on the continent' (**38**). Queen Victoria's pro-German sentiments were an embarrassment, weakening the policy of bluff that Palmerston favoured, but in 1864 the real barrier to effective action, if desired, was the French emperor's reluctance to offend Prussia to let Britain off the hook. Russell's 'unnecessarily explicit' rejection of Napoleon's proposal for a congress on Poland and Denmark and the 1815 treaties in November 1863, had caused much offence in Paris.

Palmerston had misjudged the German situation completely. Believing German unity to be impractical, he had failed to see the possibility of a dynamic relationship between German nationalism and Prussian conservatism, which Bismarck, appointed in 1862, could seek to forge (**3A**, p.47). At the time, no doubt, they seemed such unlikely bedfellows, but critics rightly attacked Palmerston and Russell for a policy of 'meddle and muddle', from which they escaped parliamentary censure by less than twenty votes. The obligation to climb down in face of force seemed to justify Cobden's assertion that henceforth 'an absolute abstention from continental politics' was Britain's only possible policy.

Britain and the United States

There was a distinct lack of harmony in Anglo-American relations for most of the nineteenth century. This seems to have been partly the legacy of the War of Independence and the brief conflict over maritime rights in 1812–14. It was also a matter of temperament. The British were regarded as haughty and old-fashioned, while most American politicians were felt to be brash and abrasive. The latter had the advantage that they could easily make political capital out of adopting an anti-British stance. British ministers on the other hand had to suffer the frustration that anti-American attitudes were not popular with the public. Although war with America was quite possible, it was unthinkable on any rational grounds. Trade and investment linked Britain to the United States; the nation was quite indifferent to the issues that annoyed ministers; Canada was also almost defenceless, so the prospect of war, when friction was very great in 1854–6, was seen by the press as the 'greatest of human calamities'.

Boundary disputes provided the most persistent cause of ill-feeling between Britain and the USA. Resentment at the existence of a British colony in North America also made the settlement of some of these disputes even more difficult. Not that the Americans had much patience with small British colonies in Central America. In the 1860s the Civil War was a major source of tension and recriminations, whereas in the 1830s and 1840s it was the slave trade that was a serious irritant.

The task of enforcing the ban on the slave trade fell mainly on the Royal Navy. Effective control necessitated a right of search and the power to arrest slavers, if caught. Even the French, who were very sensitive to the issue of maritime rights, had conceded this point in 1831–3. The Americans proved more obdurate, partly because southern slave owners were touchy about it. They also made difficulties when Palmerston tried to negotiate a 'right of visit' to check the abuse of slave traders flying the American flag. His tactless reference to the flag as merely 'a piece of bunting' brought the discussions to an end.

The Maine/New Brunswick boundary dispute dragged on until 1842, partly because the disputed territory had some strategic value to both sides and partly because local interests were strong. The high-handed treatment of a Canadian citizen in New York State in 1840 led to a threat of war by Palmerston. His successor, Aberdeen, sent out Lord Ashburton on a mission to negotiate a solution to the boundary dispute, which succeeded in reducing tension.

The Oregon boundary was a much bigger issue, because the area in dispute was so vast, embracing half of British Columbia and all of Washington, Oregon and Idaho as well as parts of two other states. At stake was the dominance of North America and the trade of the Pacific. Even Aberdeen's conciliatory approach made little headway against the assertion of America's 'Manifest Destiny' to the region, to which 5,000 American settlers migrated in 1845 compared to only 700 British. When senator Polk played politics over the issue to help his presidential election campaign, both Peel and Wellington became positively bellicose, but Aberdeen remained as conciliatory as ever. An agreement reached in June 1846 gave Vancouver Island to Britain but the rest, from the 49th parallel to the sea, went to America – a major concession on Britain's part (**13**, p. 52). The realities of the situation in America and Britain's global commitments seemingly counted for more than the validity of the claims.

The settlement of the Oregon boundary had been delayed by the Americans' suspicion of Britain having designs on Texas, (which broke away from the Mexican empire in 1836) and California. San Francisco was regarded as an excellent port but the British government was quite realistic about its chances. Texas offered opportunities for trade, but an ambitious Anglo-French plan in 1844 to cooperate over Texas was wrecked by disputes over Morocco and Tahiti. In the end, Britain gave way over both California and Texas and even refrained from fishing in troubled waters during the Mexico war in 1848.

Palmerston's fierce attack on Aberdeen for sacrificing Britain's interests and rights in the 1842 Ashburton–Webster treaty, did not inhibit him from negotiating the Clayton–Bulwer treaty of 1850. The aim was to limit American expansion into Central America by a sort of mutual self-denying agreement regarding colonization and to cooperate over a canal at Panama (**3A**, p.56). Recriminations surfaced shortly after the treaty was signed with assertions that Britain was obliged to withdraw from most of the region, regardless of her commitments to local Indians. Friction persisted through the 1850s but Palmerston was denied the showdown he desired with the Americans. Eventually, better relations were restored and Britain abandoned its protection over the Mosquito Coast and Bay Islands in 1859–60.

In Mexico, Britain and Spain agreed to participate with France in a debt collecting expedition in December 1861. Once the original objective was achieved in April 1862, Britain and Spain withdrew. France, however, which had political ambitions in Mexico, became drawn more deeply into the tangle of Mexican affairs, leading to a confrontation with the United States.

The American Civil War from 1861–5 was a dangerous time for Anglo-American relations. Although Britain pursued an official policy of neutrality, Palmerston was delighted at the prospect of the break up of the Union, while Gladstone and Russell were supporters of the South. Most 'democrats' in Britain backed the North in its campaign to defend the Union and abolish slavery. The cabinet wisely decided on a policy of 'wait and see' (**12**, p.115). European mediation was advocated by France in the course of 1862, but the British government, cautiously awaiting signs of a southern victory, refused to join with France and Russia in pressing for an armistice, despite the precaution of an Anglo-French agreement to present a united front in the event of incidents with the North. While the North took offence at British recognition of the South as belligerents, the latter was critical of Britain's policy of non-intervention.

Two incidents created serious tension in relations with the North. In late 1861 two Southern delegates were arrested on the high seas while travelling in a British mail steamer the *Trent*, a dubious, if not illegal, act which outraged public opinion. Under threat of prompt retaliation, the North wisely released the Confederate politicians. In the *Alabama* affair, the British foreign secretary was at fault in failing to halt the release in July 1862 of a new warship destined for the southern states, as neutrality implied. The *Alabama* did much damage to Northern shipping during the war, leading to a valid, albeit inflated, claim for damages against Britain. In 1871, under Gladstone's premiership, the government agreed to arbitration which, after excluding the claim for indirect damages through the alleged prolongation of the war, came up with a figure of $15 million, half of which, however, was payable to Canada. By the end of the war in 1865, American opinion was very anti-British and the United States was now a much more formidable military and naval power than previously. In 1871, it was decided to withdraw the British garrisons from Canada, whose defence against a serious American attack seemed problematic. The 'overbearing insolence' of America's political leaders was something the governments of Britain and France would have to learn to live with.

4

The Gladstone–Disraeli era, 1866–85

Britain, Prussia and the European balance of power (1866–71)

The rapid rise of Prussia–Germany to a position of diplomatic and military dominance on the continent by 1871 was clearly the main change in the balance of power in Europe between 1865 and 1885. Palmerston and Russell's gamble that Prussia could be deterred from attacking Denmark in 1864 by mere diplomatic bluff was soon made to appear ludicrous. This change is a testimony to Bismarck's diplomatic skill and the efficiency of the Prussian army and its general staff, not to mention its train drivers who made possible the rapid movement of troops to the battlefront. More seriously, it is also a reminder that Bismarck was operating in an unusually favourable diplomatic situation, especially with regard to the 'flanking powers' Russia and Britain.

Russia's adoption of a 'revisionist' stance towards European affairs, with the aim of exploiting suitable opportunities to revise the humiliating Black Sea clauses of the Treaty of Paris, initially favoured Napoleon III. The Polish revolt of 1863, however, reminded the tsar that 'Germany was the road to Poland' for a French army seeking to offer aid to the Poles. Prussia was therefore a desirable bastion and ally. Friendship with Prussia implied abandoning 'dualism' in Germany, by which the tsar had held the balance between Habsburg and

Hohenzollern pretensions to dominate the German Confederation, set up in 1815. Bismarck was the lucky beneficiary of this sea change in Russian diplomacy.

British ministers, it might be argued, lacking the gift of hindsight, too readily assumed that there was no need for Britain to try to influence the course of events between 1866 and 1871. The rise of Prussia was regarded as no real threat to British interests – providing Britain's earlier concern for the balance of power in Europe (the 'just equilibrium' of 1815) was discarded. Even Clarendon, the Liberal foreign secretary, who was more European-minded than Lord Stanley, his Conservative successor, suggested that the Austro-Prussian dispute was a quarrel between bandits that was not worth risking English blood or money to defuse. Mediation by a third power seemed to him a good idea – providing the task did not fall to Britain. Once Stanley took over the foreign office in June 1866, following the defeat of the parliamentary reform bill introduced by the Liberal government, intervention in continental politics became almost unthinkable (**16**, p. 107; **31**, p. 18).

If British ministers no longer cared about 'Europe', they seemingly cared even less about the victims of Prussian militarism. Austria was castigated by Gladstone as a 'foe to freedom', while France was seen as a constant threat or a dangerous rival, whose conversion to Free Trade was only skin deep. When prominent figures in Victorian Britain such as Richard Cobden could proclaim: 'Free Trade is God's diplomacy, and there is no other certain way of uniting people in bonds of peace', it is no wonder that God-fearing folk lost their sense of reality. More to the point, perhaps, was Cobden's assertion in 1864 that 'we have not the material strength to protect the weak against the strong'.

The lack of a large army was obviously an inhibiting factor in the later 1860s, but the lack of will to exercise diplomatic influence seems to have been the crucial factor from June 1866 to December 1868 when Stanley was foreign secretary. Despite friendly warnings, he made non-intervention so strong a feature of Britain's foreign policy that her policy in any situation was almost totally predictable. This was even made explicit in a statement to parliament in 1866 that 'ours will be a pacific policy, a policy of observation rather than action'. This was obviously a very different approach from that of Palmerston.

Clarendon was more francophile (pro-French) than most of his contemporaries but this does not seem to have made much difference in practice.

The danger in all this, as the queen's private secretary noted in August 1866, was that while it made sense to avoid being mixed up in some of these continental troubles, 'it will hardly do for England to stand so completely aloof . . . and to abdicate her position as one of the great European powers'. It was still possible for Britain to take diplomatic initiatives, or even to respond positively to others', despite her relative lack of military strength. Lord Salisbury, Conservative foreign secretary in 1878, questioned Britain's failure to react to the Prussian demand for Alsace–Lorraine in September 1870, by asking: 'Has it really come to this, that the disposal of the frontiers of France and Germany is a matter to us of purest unconcern? Is not the crisis worth some little risk?' (**16**, p. 212).

This seems to be the sort of case argued by Agatha Ramm in her discussion of Liberal foreign policy. She claims that as late as the summer of 1870 Britain still exercised a sort of ascendancy even if this was partly 'by default'. With France absorbed in Napoleon III's major constitutional changes (the Liberal Empire), Austria–Hungary trying to implement changes to her political structure, and Russia still engrossed in modernization, Britain 'looked like the strongest international force', at least until it was put to the test with the outbreak of the Franco-Prussian war in July 1870 (**3B**, p. 85).

In September 1870, the French army was humbled at the disaster of Sedan, bringing to an ignominious end Napoleon III's Second Empire. In the following spring, the German Empire was proclaimed in the palace of Versailles, symbol of French glory under Louis XIV. Bismarck's three wars, against the Danes, the Austrians and the French, made Prussia–Germany the dominant military power on the continent, with all that that implied.

British ministers, however, seemed singularly unmoved by the rise of Germany even though it was accomplished through a combination of Prussian militarism with Bismarckian *Realpolitik*. In part this was a reaction to Palmerston and Russell's policy of bluff, of 'menaces never accomplished', in their vain attempt to provide diplomatic aid (not backed by force) to the Danes in the Schleswig–Holstein affair. In part, it was also a sign of insularity – a preoccupation with domestic issues, especially the intricate details of parliamentary reform in 1866 and 1867.

The growing tension between Austria and Prussia in 1866 could be dismissed as a quarrel between the two German powers and therefore of no direct concern to Britain, especially as the root cause seemed to be a dispute over the disposal of their ill-gotten gains, the Danish duchies. Clarendon privately suggested that Europe would be glad to see Prussia getting a licking by the Austrians – a view not shared by his Conservative successor.

The scale of Austria's defeat in 1866 was not anticipated even by Napoleon III, for whom an enlarged and more powerful Prussia was a serious threat – hence the comment by critics of the Emperor that 'It was France that was beaten at Sadowa.' If British ministers misjudged the outcome as well, they could be forgiven for not seeing the significance of an event that did not seem to touch directly on British interests. The fact that Anglo-French relations remained cool, following their disagreements in the crises over Poland and Denmark in 1863–4, made concerted action to defuse the tension in 1866 less likely, though it was not for want of trying on Napoleon's part.

The growth of tension between Prussia and France from 1867 to 1870 was, arguably, something that was of serious concern to Britain. Napoleon's scheme to obtain Luxembourg by purchase from the king of Holland was a harmless enough project designed to placate French public opinion for Prussia's expansion. Bismarck, however, went back on his tacit acceptance of the deal, alleging German national sentiment as a new factor to be reckoned with. Only a conference could produce the essential face-saving compromise in 1867, but Stanley came close to wrecking it by his persistent reluctance to accept the need for a guarantee of the duchy's independence as a way of resolving the crisis.

None of the British foreign secretaries of this period were a match for Bismarck. His skilful manoeuvring to secure acceptance of a Hohenzollern prince as king of Spain, thereby presenting France with a *fait accompli* that she could not accept with honour, was too astute for them. While Stanley naively believed that Bismarck was 'one of the surest guarantees for peace that we have', Clarendon, back at the foreign office in December 1868, was not even aware of the Hohenzollern candidacy until March 1870. Granville, who took over after Clarendon's death in June 1870, allowed his sense of propriety and tact to blunt his initiative in the crisis. Not surprisingly, therefore, the war came as a shock to the British government in July 1870 and Bismarck's publication of the evidence of France's ambitions towards Belgium in 1866 served to confirm British suspicions of the French (**3B**, 16).

A powerful argument in favour of non-intervention in continental affairs was the relative weakness of the British army. With only 20,000 men available for active service out of a total of less than 90,000 stationed at home, such an army was not a force to be reckoned with. Prussia had a peacetime force of 300,000 with reserves of twice that figure, while France could put 400,000 men into the field with half as many in reserve. Britain's naval power was obviously not of much use in a Franco-Prussian war.

The commonest argument in 1870 was probably the selfish view that a Prussian victory did not constitute a threat to British interests. Rather the reverse, since a strong Germany would act as a bulwark against France. Why a bulwark might be needed against a defeated France was not considered. Clarendon, who died two weeks before the outbreak of the war, was almost alone in his pro-French sympathies, while the Queen displayed her usual partisanship for her German relatives.

Both the decline of the Concert of Europe, following the Crimean war, and the reluctance to stand by the concept of the balance of power were significant factors in the diplomacy of the later 1860s. Russia's 'revisionist' stance after 1856 and her abandonment of the role of defender of the *status quo* in Europe created opportunities for ambitious policies by France, and later, Prussia. As the Prince Napoleon observed in April 1869: 'the old public law has disappeared and has not yet been replaced by any new law of nations'. Thiers, seeking sympathetic support for France's plight after her defeat, lamented in a famous phrase, that he could no longer find Europe.

Non-intervention nevertheless had its dangers, despite the insistence of the Manchester School of Cobden and Bright that the 'foul idol' of the balance of power should be destroyed in favour of a policy of 'no foreign politics'. What these critics failed to appreciate was, as the Committee of Imperial Defence emphasised in July 1920, that 'We cannot be free to carry out our main objects, which are imperial and colonial, unless we are safe in Europe'. Security in Europe depended, in part, on the continued existence of that 'just equilibrium' on the continent which the critics derided. Stanley's 'wimpish' approach to foreign affairs did Britain no good, resulting in the almost total effacement of England in the eyes of Europe. By proclaiming too loudly Britain's indifference to the events on the continent he ensured that by the end of 1867 Britain had been written off. A year earlier she had been judged capable of influencing the Franco-Prussian issue (**16**, p. 225). The queen made the point emphatically in 1867 when Belgium seemed at risk, arguing that 'England must show the World that she is not prepared to abdicate her position as a great Power. . . .' Disraeli had made a similar case in 1859 in his reporting of France's view that 'by not taking part in the Italian war, we have sunk into a second-rate Power'.

In this period both parliament and public opinion seemed averse to Britain taking risks through involvement in continental affairs, an attitude perilously close to isolationism. Ministers not only resented the loss of parliamentary time devoted to discussion of foreign affairs, but even feared that fragile majorities might disintegrate if foreign policy were debated too passionately. Hence the insistence by the government of the day that such matters did not affect British interests. Perhaps the best defence of a cautious approach was the surprising assertion made by Clarendon in May 1869 that 'It is the unfriendly state of our relations with America that to a great extent paralyses our action in Europe.' By 1871, however, there were signs of a turning of the tide in public opinion when the Liberal government was attacked for its apparent indifference to the crushing defeat of France.

'Gladstonism' and 'Beaconsfieldism' in foreign affairs

The swings of the political pendulum in 1874 and 1880 provide an opportunity to note the contrasting approaches to international affairs of Gladstone and Disraeli (later Lord Beaconsfield). If this does not represent a precise comparison of Liberal and Conservative foreign policy in the period 1868 to 1885, it is partly because both premiers pursued a rather idiosyncratic, highly personal, line in diplomacy. It was also partly because of the relationship between the prime ministers and their foreign secretaries. For instance, Disraeli became very impatient with the opposition of Derby (the former Lord Stanley) to his proposals for anti-Russian measures. His resignation and replacement by Salisbury in 1878 removed much of this tension. The relationship between Gladstone and Granville was, Agatha Ramm suggests, a constructive one during his first ministry (1868–74) with the sceptical Granville acting as a useful brake on some of Gladstone's enthusiasms, though much less so in 1880–5 (**3B**, p. 86).

Gladstone did not belong to the non-interventionist camp or allow Cobdenite doctrine to determine British policy, but he was a great believer in 'Thatcherite' sound finance – the sort of rigorous fiscal policies pursued by Tory governments in the years 1979–97. His addiction to retrenchment (cutting public expenditure – mostly on the armed forces) weakened Britain's ability to play the role of a great power which his love of peace tended to circumscribe anyway. In addition, Gladstone's enthusiasm for domestic reform could prevent him from paying attention to serious situations overseas, as in 1884.

'Gladstonism' was idealism rampant, combined in a curious way with a strong legalistic vein. Foreign policy ought not to be about the pursuit of power, he believed, but the rule of law applied to international affairs. Gladstone also displayed a touching belief in the Concert of Europe as a mechanism for realising the new era in international affairs that he naively believed possible in an age characterised by *Realpolitik*. The shortcomings in 'Gladstonism' were not so apparent in the years 1868–74 as they became later. Faced with the issues of the *Alabama* dispute with the USA, the Franco-Prussian war, and the repudiation by Russia of the Black Sea clauses of the Treaty of Paris, 'Gladstonism' was possibly a not inappropriate response for a government engrossed in domestic reform (**3B**, p. 20).

Britain was in the wrong over the *Alabama* affair so the payment of damages was almost unavoidable. It therefore made sense to adopt a conciliatory stance and even, as Gladstone suggested, to express regret for the incident, thereby facilitating the reopening of the negotiations. By offering a review of all claims between Britain and the USA it became easier to make concessions and reach compromises. The most difficult problem was the issue of 'indirect claims' – the Americans alleging that the *Alabama*'s attacks resulted in a prolongation of the war.

The arbitration award of £3 million damages in 1872 was a set back for the Liberal government but was accepted for the sake of the principle of submitting disputes to arbitration, rather than go to war.

The outbreak of the Franco-Prussian war in July 1870 took the foreign office by surprise. British opinion blamed France for over reacting to Bismarck's provocative conduct in the affair of the 'Prussian' candidate for the Spanish throne. This made it easier for Gladstone and Granville to make respect for Belgium's neutrality their key concern. Securing guarantees from both sides satisfied the demands of 'legalism' and provided a substitute for a policy, which was comforting for a time. The shock came with the announcement that Prussia intended to demand the cession of Alsace–Lorraine. This was a grave infringement of Gladstone's belief in self-determination, but Granville's insistence that Britain had no power to stop it won the backing of the cabinet. The government could try to justify its refusal to attempt mediation, requested by the French, on the grounds that Prussia's victory was not harmful to British interests, but Britain's role in the war began to seem ignoble by the spring of 1871, when public opinion turned against Prussia.

Britain's standing as a great power had already taken a buffeting from Russia's decision to exploit a favourable opportunity to denounce the Black Sea clauses of the Treaty of Paris, in November 1870. This action offended Gladstone's sense of what was legal in international affairs and led him to insist on the summoning of a conference which duly produced a protocol condemning the unilateral denunciation of treaties. At least Granville had succeeded in enlisting Bismarck's support for a congress, so demonstrating that Prussia was not backing Russia in an expansionist policy. Was there a viable alternative to acquiescence? The other signatories to the tripartite convention of 1856 to defend the Treaty of Paris were in no mood for a crisis, but public opinion, accustomed to regarding Russia as an enemy of the British Empire, felt let down. The conference may have been more than just a face saver, but not very clearly so (then or now). Gladstone's sensible solution was noticeably lacking in Palmerstonian panache.

The Gladstone government was vulnerable to taunts of weakness and truckling to foreigners, notably the Russians and the Americans, to the detriment of British prestige. In some ways the years 1868–74 could be regarded as continuing the drift in foreign policy and downward slide of British power since 1865, even if Gladstone was not a committed non-interventionist like Lord Stanley in 1866–7. Evaluating the conduct of British foreign policy from 1868 to 1874 is quite difficult. Was Gladstone's conciliatory approach towards the problems of the *Alabama* claim and the Black Sea clauses an eminently sensible policy or did it signify that Britain played an ignominious role in her dealings with America and Russia? Disraeli obviously stressed the latter in his attacks on Gladstone's foreign policy and the theme has naturally been widely used in critiques of the achievements of the Liberals from 1868 to 1874. Taking a broader view, Bourne welcomes the appointment of Salisbury as foreign secretary in 1878 on the grounds that it 'freed England from the sterile policies of [both] Granville and Derby' (**13**, p. 133; **20**, p. 19).

That Britain's voice counted for more in Europe by 1880 seems undeniable. This was probably because Disraeli seemed to be aware of the importance of great power relationships, of which Gladstone was said to be 'wholly ignorant'. He correctly saw that Prussia's defeat of France in 1871 meant that 'The balance of power has been entirely destroyed', adding that 'There is not a diplomatic tradition which has not been swept away.' Granville's seeming lack of concern for the fate of France in 1871 made him vulnerable to the charge of pursuing a 'policy of selfish isolation'. Disraeli also understood the importance of prestige in European affairs, which the Liberals ignored, as well as the appeal of patriotism (**25**).

Disraeli was no idealist. He was an opportunist, pursuing whatever policy seemed expedient at the time, with an eye to prestige successes – just like a 'foreigner', as Derby alleged in snobbish fashion. Showmanship came naturally to him, as is suggested by Punch cartoons of the period. But Disraeli grasped the important fact that self-assertion was a necessary attribute for a nation in the Bismarck era.

In making the break up of the *Dreikaiserbund* (Three Emperors' League) his main aim during the early stages of the Near East crisis, Disraeli showed he had grasped the need to restore some flexibility to great power alignments after 1871, if Britain was to play a leading part in Europe. His determination to stand up to Russia, even to the point of threatening war, may have been based on a misreading of Russia's official foreign policy, but it restored Britain to a position of some importance in European affairs. The role played by Salisbury and Disraeli at the Congress of Berlin in 1878 demonstrated this well.

His Palmerstonian touch was evident in the Abyssinian campaign in 1867 – a rescue mission to save the lives of British officials. His references to the theme of empire in his Crystal Palace speech of 1872 may have been kite-flying but the imperial idea caught the public imagination and seemed to be an electoral asset for the Tory party for the next thirty years. Even the disasters that resulted from 'forward' policies in Afghanistan and South Africa were followed by military successes to vindicate British arms.

Disraeli (unlike Gladstone) knew how to pander to the queen, who responded (rather too?) eagerly to the idea of being endowed with the title Empress of India. The Royal Titles Bill of 1876 possibly indicated special insight into oriental attitudes on Disraeli's part as a means of fostering Indian loyalty to their own 'Empress', engaged in a prestige battle with the Tsar-Emperor of Russia. Purchasing the khedive's shares in the Suez Canal in 1875 certainly prevented the French getting control of a vital artery to the east and made the undiscerning Briton believe that the canal now belonged to England, thanks to Disraeli's flamboyant action. As Lord Beaconsfield (Disraeli's reward for the Empress title according to Mr Punch – on the basis of 'one good turn deserves another') the premier was held responsible for the failure of warlike policies in South Africa and Afghanistan. The resultant bloodshed and expenditure of these military adventures, attacked by Gladstone as evidence of moral decline and an excess in imperial spirit, were laid at the door of 'Beaconsfieldism'.

Despite the justice of such criticism, the fact remains that British prestige in Europe was higher in 1880 than in 1874. Yet by 1885, according to Ramm, Gladstone and Granville had reduced Britain to being on a par with Italy as 'the least of the Great Powers', the appearance (however illusory) of her ascendancy in 1870 having been reversed.

Disraeli and the Near East crisis (1875–8)

Disraeli's triumphant return from the Congress of Berlin in 1878, claiming to have secured 'Peace with Honour', marked the high point of his statesmanship. He seemed to have achieved a lot: Russia gave way over the issue of a greatly enlarged Bulgarian state, while Britain acquired Cyprus as a base for defending Asiatic Turkey. The Panslavist dream of Holy Russia occupying Constantinople had been resisted. In the long term, however, propping up the Ottoman Empire may have been, as Salisbury later conceded, a case of backing the wrong horse.

If Disraeli's handling of the crisis in the Balkans was a success, luck played a significant part in it. The evidence suggests that he had no clear strategy for dealing with the crises that arose but relied on a series of improvisations that eventually worked out in his favour. Disraeli's skill lay in surmounting a number of setbacks that could have proved fatal to his policy.

The growing rift with his foreign secretary, who colluded with the Russian ambassador by passing on cabinet information, made decision-making difficult. Derby's motives were honourable – he was intent on preserving peace – and he may even have prevented an unnecessary war, but his action intensified cabinet disagreements. He also dismissed overtures from Bismarck in early 1876 without much discussion (3). The swings in public opinion, especially the anti-Turk phase in late 1876–7, caused Disraeli problems, while palace revolutions made the sultan's political capacity and Turkish military capability very hard to evaluate. The enormous gulf between the modest aims of official Russian policy and the heady dreams of Panslav enthusiasts (some occupying important diplomatic or military posts) made it difficult to gauge Russia's true intentions.

The clue to Disraeli's initial attitude to the Balkan problem was his desire to break up the cosy *Dreikaiserbund* club of Germany, Austria and Russia that left Britain no room for manoeuvre. Hence his rejection of Austro-Russian solutions to the crisis, devised without consultation with Britain. The crisis, however, simply worsened with time. The revolt against Turkish rule in Bosnia in 1875 spread to Bulgaria in 1876, which was fiercely suppressed, and led to intervention by Serbia (with Panslav backing) whose designs on Bosnia worried the Austrians until the Turkish defeat of the Serbs in September 1876.

Disraeli's pro-Turkish stance led him to reject both the Andrassy Note, an Austrian plan for a series of modest reforms in Bosnia, and its successor, the Berlin Memorandum entailing more sweeping reforms. This negative approach was undermined by the news of the Bulgarian Atrocities. Western press reports not only ignored the massacres of Muslims by Bulgars but also greatly exaggerated the scale of the 'Atrocities' committed by the ill-disciplined Turkish irregulars, pressed into service by a regime whose best troops were tied up in Bosnia and elsewhere. Disraeli's denial of the Bulgarian atrocities, based on misleading information from diplomatic sources, left him vulnerable to a broadside from Gladstone, whose pamphlet, published in September 1876, stirred public opinion against the Turks.

Fearful of a Russian move against Constantinople, Disraeli cast around for a policy that would preserve the sultan's independence. The Constantinople Conference (December 1876) and the London Protocol of March 1877 amounted to little more than playing for time. The Russian declaration of war on Turkey in late April 1877, confirmed Disraeli's worst fears, but the premier could not persuade the cabinet of the need for a dramatic move – such as seizing the Dardanelles. As he explained to the outraged queen: 'there were not three men' in the cabinet who favoured declaring war on Russia.

The gallant defence of the fortress of Plevna swung public opinion in Britain back in favour of the 'heroic little Turk'. Its fall in December 1877 and the renewed Russian advance to Adrianople revived fears of a march on the Turkish capital. An armistice was followed by the treaty of San Stephano in March 1878 which caused a major crisis. The creation of Greater Bulgaria under Russian influence all but eliminated Turkey in Europe, while Serbia, Montenegro, and Roumania were to become fully independent. In addition, Russia made some useful gains in Asiatic Turkey. The tension in Anglo-Russian relations rose to new heights exemplified, by a music hall song which ended with the line 'The Russians shall not have CON–STAN–TI–NO–PLE'. 'Jingoism' was born, and worsened when the Russians proved reluctant to submit the whole of their Panslav-inspired treaty to scrutiny by the other powers.

Disraeli seized his chance. Ignoring Derby's 'purposeless vacillation', as Salisbury termed it, he secured a vote of war credits and ordered the fleet to the Dardanelles. When the Russians prevaricated, the government called out the Reserves and summoned troops from India to Malta. Salisbury, though sceptical about Britain's 'outmoded' pro Turk policy, began to doubt Russia's good faith. His Circular in April 1878 arguing the case for treaty revision, seconded the Austrian demand for a conference, won Bismarck's approval, and enabled Russia to give way gracefully.

The success of the Congress of Berlin in the summer of 1878 was partly due to pre-conference negotiations which established a basis of agreement on key issues, particularly between Britain and Russia. It also owed quite a lot to Bismarck's ruthless chairmanship, forcing the weaker states to give way. Cooperation between Britain and Austria–Hungary kept up the pressure on Russia. Disraeli's performance at the congress was something of a personal triumph, partly because he was dissuaded from making his main speech in French, in which his fluency was not as good as he imagined.

Greater Bulgaria, intended as a Russian satellite, was split in three, but the artificial semi-autonomous state of Eastern Rumelia lasted less than a decade. The return of an ethnically mixed 'Macedonia' to full Turkish rule was an unhappy decision for its inhabitants, but it preserved a viable-sized European Turkey until the Balkan wars of 1912–13. The view of some historians that the Balkans should have been left under Russian domination contains too many imponderables for serious debate (**33**, p. 253; **10**, p. 123–4). The Austrian 'occupation' of Bosnia–Herzegovina created much animosity, not least with the sultan, who also resented the British acquisition of Cyprus despite the guarante of Turkey in Asia, which subsequently proved unworkable. Disraeli, however, had some reason to feel pleased with the outcome of the crisis. He had split the *Dreikaiserbund* and encouraged Austria–Hungary turn to Britain for support. In addition, the British position in the Mediterranean and the route to the East had been made secure. As A. J. P. Taylor suggested in a rather neat assessment, 'Great Britain won a bloodless victory with a music-hall song, (and) a navy of museum pieces . . .' (**33**, p. 250) – a better outcome to a Near East crisis, at least, than the Crimean War.

Britain, Afghanistan and South Africa (1874–85)

There is no evidence that when Disraeli came to power in 1874 he intended to abandon the cautious approach of the the Liberals and embark on 'forward' policies in Africa and Central Asia. The fact that his government became responsible for wars in both Afghanistan and South Africa was partly bad luck. He was not well-served by two of his ministers who preferred deer hunting or claret drinking to close attention to their departmental duties. Worse still was the headstrong behaviour of the key 'Men on the Spot'. The combination was fatal. As Disraeli's biographer says: 'in an era of slow communications and an ill-coordinated governmental machine, it was not at all easy to control those high officers of state . . . described as "prancing proconsuls"'. The appointment of Lytton, a minor diplomat, 'a man of gaudy and theatrical ambition', to the post of Viceroy of India was a case of bad judgement by Disraeli. The choice of Frere as Governor of the Cape was not much better, since he persisted with his notion that the Zulus had to be destroyed as a warrior race, despite orders to proceed with caution. Confronted with crises and military set-backs, the government in London faced the dilemma of disavowing imprudent actions or defending British prestige (**25**).

Russian expansion across Central Asia in the 1860s and 1870s was in part a response to the setbacks in the Near East in 1856. It was a possible threat to the security of India, since the independence of Persia and Afghanistan, 'the walls of the Indian garden', seemed to be endangered as a consequence of the Russian occupation of Tashkent, Samarkand and then Khiva (in 1873).

In 1873 the Liberal government decided against a direct approach to the Persians and Afghans in favour of a 'hands off' agreement with Russia. This meant treating the river Oxus as the frontier of Afghanistan which, as an independent state, could act as a buffer between the expanding Russian empire and British India. By this decision the Gladstone government committed itself to the 'masterly inactivity' school of sitting behind defensible frontiers, as opposed to the 'forward' school, which advocated advancing the frontiers with the aid of strategic railways and establishing British influence over regions such as Afghanistan (**14**, pp. 78–9).

Lytton belonged to the forward school and decided to interpret his instructions in that sense when he was appointed Viceroy of India in 1876. This was slightly odd since Salisbury, at the India Office before he became Foreign Secretary in 1878, favoured a defensive posture in Central Asia, doubting the feasibility of a Russian attack on India. But it was Salisbury's earlier concern to keep the Russians out of Kabul that gave Lytton some excuse to press the amir to allow more British influence over his policy.

Lytton miscalculated. The amir feared that the main threat to his independence came from the British, so he agreed to a Russian mission at Kabul, followed by a treaty, in the summer of 1878, at a time when the Russians anticipated war over Bulgaria. After the Congress of Berlin, however, negotiations between London and St. Petersburg were likely to succeed in securing the withdrawal of the Russian mission. Lytton's advance (contrary to instructions) to the Khyber Pass in September 1878 was halted by the amir's refusal to accept a British mission at Kabul, which was regarded as a snub, to be avenged. The military expedition under General Roberts went well and resulted in the Treaty of Gandamak, but in September 1879 it all went wrong. The murder of the British Resident at Kabul was followed by a defeat at Maiwand and the siege of a British force at Kandahar. These disasters led to a new campaign by General Roberts to avenge British honour, and another treaty negotiated by the newly-elected Liberal government restoring Afghan independence, but retaining British control of the Khyber Pass. The Russians were happy to back off from a confrontation in Central Asia in 1879–80, when all was quiet in the Near East.

Gladstone had attacked Disraeli for pursuing a 'baseless quarrel' with the amir, in the course of his Midlothian campaign, with much stress on the moral aspects as well as the loss of life. After the 1880 election he abandoned the forward policy and (less justifiably) stopped the building of a strategic railway to Quetta. The flaw in Liberal policy was revealed, however, in 1884 when the Russians annexed Merv, in contravention of a promise made in 1881. Herat seemed now at risk, so a restart had to be made on the Quetta railway.

There was worse to follow. In March 1885 Russian forces clashed with Afghan troops at Penjdeh, creating a major crisis in Anglo-Russian relations. Even Gladstone felt it necessary to make a stand, insisting that the Zulficar Pass be denied to the Russians. Salisbury, on becoming premier, sought Germany's neutrality for a showdown with Russia but the crisis ended in September 1885 when the Zulficar Pass was restored to Afghan control, even though a new crisis was beginning over Bulgaria.

The moral seemed to be that Britain should place its trust in the Afghans' love of their own independence, but not trust the Russians to keep their promises. As Salisbury drily observed in 1885: 'It was not wise to seek as the main object of our policy to rest the defence of India upon the guarantee of Russia . . . we must do it ourselves.' (14, p. 88). Negotiations with Russia were not very profitable. There was no need for her to make concessions in Asia where the British Empire was at its most vulnerable, since warships could not sail up the Khyber Pass to defend the North-West Frontier. General Roberts seemed to have got it right in his comment that 'the less the Afghans see of us, the more they like us.'

African affairs were only just beginning to require the attention of British governments in the 1870s. South Africa, on the other hand, had been a sensitive issue for decades because of the strategic importance of the Cape for the route to India, which the opening of the Suez Canal in 1869 did little to diminish. The British government wanted to secure peace and stability in South Africa but at the lowest possible cost – a commonplace of colonial policy. This was not easy when a struggle for supremacy among the African peoples in the region was complicated by the presence of the land hungry Boers, whose dislike of English rule was very strong.

Colonial secretaries of the period were bemused by the potential of 'federation' as a magic solution to the problem partly because it had recently been attempted in Canada with some success. The belligerent Boers of the Transvaal were persuaded to agree to annexation by Britain in April 1877, through fear of being wiped out by the Zulus, resentful of the rough treatment they received at the hands of white mercenaries. Sir Bartle Frere, an experienced official recently transferred from India, did not allow his ignorance of African affairs to influence his judgement in insisting on disarming the Zulus. Despite London's disapproval of his 'forward' policy, the government sent troop reinforcements, but over 1500 men were killed at the battle of Isandhlwana in January 1879, through neglect of the simple defensive precautions that were used to great effect by another British force at Rorke's Drift. To avenge this disaster more troops had to be sent out, defeating the Zulus at Ulundi.

The casualties and the expense of the military operations left Disraeli's government very vulnerable to the charge of inciting an inglorious and costly war, with the moral issue given much prominence by Gladstone in the 1880 election campaign. Once in power, however, the Liberal government hesitated to reverse Disraeli's policy, hoping to persist with the policy of federation. But, with the Zulu threat kindly removed by Britain, the Transvaal Boers became impatient to recover their independence and clashed with a British force at Majuba Hill in 1881. The press demanded revenge for this slight to British arms in the so-called 'first Boer war', but Gladstone preferred negotiation. In the Pretoria Convention of 1881, the Transvaal regained its independence but with Britain having control over its foreign policy. This later became highly contentious. Gladstone's legacy was unfortunate. The imperial government in London was shown to be indecisive and unreliable, but ready to make concessions to the use of force.

A more glaring case of misjudgement was Granville's lack of response to Bismarck's repeated enquiries in 1883–4 about the status of South-West Africa. Convinced that Bismarck still adhered to his openly anti-colonialist stance of 1881 (as most of his utterances implied) Granville saw no urgency in returning a precise or prompt reply to Berlin. His casual attitude was reinforced by delays in decision-making by the Cape government, which wanted to annex the region but without the expense of administering it. When Bismarck's impatience (feigned or real?) with these twists and evasions ran out in June 1884 (conveniently in time for the German elections) the British government, facing problems over Egypt, not only gave way over South-West Africa but also meekly accepted Germany's other brusquely presented claims to protectorates over Togo, the Kameruns, and East Africa.

The humiliation continued when Bismarck, confident of French support, rejected Britain's dubious treaty with Portugal as a barrier to European penetration of the Congo. After the Berlin West Africa Conference (November 1884 to February 1885) had resolved rival claims to territory in Africa, Bismarck, feeling well satisfied with the outcome on the colonial and the electoral front, was willing to accept Britain's proposals for dealing with the problem of Egypt's finances (14).

Gladstone, Egypt and the Sudan (1880–5)

There is a double irony in the fact that the decision to occupy

Egypt in 1882 was made by such an avowed 'anti-imperialist' as Gladstone and that the outcome was to alienate Republican France, the natural ally of liberal England, for over twenty years. The Anglo-French Dual Control system had been set up in 1876 to bring order to Egypt's finances after the khedive's declaration of bankruptcy. Resentment at interference by foreigners, Turks as well as Europeans, fuelled a nationalist movement and led to some unrest. Serious riots at Alexandria in June 1882 in which about fifty Europeans were killed, increased the demand for intervention in Egypt to restore order.

The sultan refused to exercise his rights as suzerain to send in Turkish troops, as Gladstone wished, while the French vetoed his second idea of inviting the other great powers, acting as the European Concert, to replace the Dual Control. The Liberal government received alarming reports from the British consul-general and others (the 'Men on the Spot') that not only were European financial interests at risk but that the Suez Canal itself was in danger. What was to be done?

Explanations of the curious decision to occupy Egypt tend to focus on either the strategic motive or the financial – or even a mixture of both. The classic example of the former is that given by Robinson and Gallagher in '*Africa and the Victorians*', over thirty years ago (4). They portray Gladstone and Granville as determined not to go beyond diplomatic moves, resisting French pressure for a military expedition, as implied in the Joint Note of January 1882. 'Egypt for the Egyptians' may have been Gladstone's motto, but for the Whigs in his cabinet the security of the route to India was of prime importance (**14**, p. 50). By contrast, the influence of financial considerations on British policy in 1882 has been stressed in a recent contribution to the debate by A. G. Hopkins. He asserts that 'The disorder they feared was financial; and fiscal anarchy was a moral issue, not just an economic one'. The crux of the matter, he suggests, was the reluctance of the British government to concede control over the budget to the Egyptians in the 1880s, when Britain's economic stake in the country was thought to be worth defending (**5**, p. 368).

But Gladstone and Chamberlain are normally credited with feeling sympathy for the rights of the Egyptian people. What worried them was that the leadership of the nationalist movement was in the hands of an allegedly authoritarian clique of army officers under Arabi Pasha, which smacked of adventurism. Other members of Gladstone's cabinet pressed hard for a firm line to be taken in the crisis, either to ensure the safety of the route to India or for the sake of British prestige in general. Cabinet disunity, which might bring about the fall of the government and jeopardise the Liberal 'programme', was another factor in the situation.

Faced with 'nothing but bad alternatives to choose from' as Granville put it, Gladstone reluctantly agreed to allow Admiral Seymour to carry out the bombardment of Alexandria that was deemed vital to destroy Arabi's new fortifications around the port. A week later, on about 20 July, the order was given to prepare an expeditionary force to be sent to Egypt, which defeated Arabi's army at Tel el Kebir in mid-September 1882.

Despite numerous statements of intent, Britain did not withdraw from Egypt, even though the Law of Liquidations of 1880 had settled the financial problems arising from the khedive's bankruptcy, to the satisfaction of the foreign bondholders at least. The sad fact was that British policy had created a power vacuum in Egypt. Arabi's movement had been destroyed by force, while the khedive's prestige had been undermined, so there was no one whom the British could entrust with the responsibility for governing the country. Or so it seemed, at least, given the importance of political stability to the issue of financial probity and the safety of the canal. A British evacuation of Egypt might also be an invitation to another power to step in. Furthermore, the beginnings of a *jihad* in the Egyptian Sudan was showing signs of becoming a threat to Egypt itself.

Gladstone's concept of a 'moral tutelage' over Egypt to assist its recovery gave a veneer of respectability to the British occupation. Not that Bismarck opposed it, seeing it as a likely source of friction between Britain and France. What angered the French was Gladstone's decision to stay in Egypt, without reviving the Dual Control. This was a blow to French pride since their cultural links (and some degree of political influence) were well established. A French historian suggested that pique at the alleged indecisiveness shown by their government in the crisis (when the French fleet was ordered to sail away from the action at Alexandria in July 1882) also aroused French opinion against Britain – a remarkable display of French logic. The estrangement had serious diplomatic consequences nonetheless.

The Liberal government failed to declare a protectorate over Egypt in 1882, which imposed severe limits on the power Britain could actually exercise. Worse still, Gladstone agreed to the creation of an international Commission of the Egyptian Public Debt in 1885, after France had sabotaged the conference on Egypt's finances the previous year. British governments therefore had the burden of administering Egypt without the freedom to use tax revenues on worthy reform projects. Germany's acquiesence was available, but at a price, usually colonial concessions – the so called *bâton égyptien*, or 'Egyptian lever'. Hence the comment by the British administrator, the future Lord Cromer, that 'Berlin and not Cairo is the real centre of gravity of Egyptian affairs'. This was evident in 1884–5 when Bismarck decided to satisfy the growing pressure in Germany for overseas colonies.

A major cause of the financial problem in Egypt in 1884 was the ongoing crisis in the Sudan. An Egyptian army under Hicks Pasha was destroyed by the rebellious forces of the Mahdi in late 1883. Evacuation of the Sudan was the only sensible course but the scattered garrisons were a difficult problem. General Gordon was sent to oversee the evacuation but after much confusion decided to ignore his instructions and use Khartoum as a focus of resistance to the Mahdists. In London the gravity of the situation seemed not to have been noticed. Gladstone was absorbed in the intricacies of a reform bill, while Granville displayed the same dilatoriness towards this crisis as he was showing over South–West Africa. Reinforcements were eventually despatched but they arrived just too late to save Gordon and his men. Public opinion, kept on tenterhooks by the press reports of the relief army's slow progress up the Nile, turned against Gladstone with some vehemence in late January 1885. The government narrowly avoided defeat on a motion of censure by a mere fourteen votes but resigned eventually in June 1885. It may well be that Bismarck was not alone in regarding Gladstone at this time as the most incompetent English minister since Lord North in 1775.

In Gladstone's defence it has to be said that his good qualities were not likely to be appreciated by the admirer of 'blood and iron' and the practitioner of *Realpolitik*. Gladstone's moral Christian stance, his support for 'peoples struggling to be free' (such as the Bulgarians) did have some admirers. His opposition to 'forward' policies was vindicated, at least in part, by Disraeli's experience of the problems of controlling 'prancing proconsuls' such as Lytton. Furthermore, the Penjdeh crisis of 1885 seemed to reveal the wisdom of allowing Afghan independence to flourish as a check to the Russians, by withdrawing British forces in 1880 (**20**). It may have been a gamble, however, since the unexpected arrival of a capable amir was a factor of some importance in Afghan affairs. Gladstone's desire for a 'common accord' of Europe was a well-meaning attempt to revive the spirit of the Concert, in decline since 1856, but it seemed inappropriate in the era of Bismarckian alliances. Above all, he epitomized a 'crusade for righteousness' in foreign policy, desirable, no doubt, on ethical grounds and creating a special affinity with the popular classes of Victorian Britain (**14**, p. 2).

On the other hand, the 'apostle of absolute negation in foreign affairs', as Salisbury described him, was prone to an excess of preaching and moralizing, for which he was dubbed the 'Mahdi of Midlothian' by his detractors. He was also regarded as incompetent in some aspects of diplomacy. Agatha Ramm criticizes his record in the period 1880–5 on the grounds: 'The Great Powers of Europe were marshalled under the ascendancy of Bismarckian Germany' (**3B**, p. 86) thus leaving Britain out in the cold, along with Republican France, whom Gladstone had succeeded in alienating over Egypt. To make matters worse, Russia was antagonized over Afghanistan, while Granville had infuriated Bismarck by his ineptitude in responding to German hints about colonies in South-West Africa in 1884.

Britain's prestige was at a low ebb in 1884–5, and the Liberals, especially Gladstone and Granville, were largely responsible for it. The jibe in the German press (probably by Bismarck) that 'The Gladstone government was the best one conceivable for all countries – with the exception of England' would almost certainly have been endorsed by Salisbury, not to mention Queen Victoria (**31**, p. 174). They had, in effect, achieved almost the impossible – a Franco-German front against Britain over the Congo and the issue of the Egyptian finances. The first led to the Berlin West Africa conference of 1884–5; the second to the failure of the London conference on Egyptian finance in 1884 at both of which Franco-German collaboration was much in evidence. No wonder Salisbury complained at the legacy of the Liberals in 1885, saying: 'They have at least achieved their long desired "Concert of Europe". They have succeeded in uniting the Continent of Europe – against England' (**13**, p. 144).

It says much for Salisbury's diplomatic skill that within a few years of his return to the Foreign Office (which he held jointly with the premiership), he had out-manoeuvred Russia over the union of Bulgaria and Eastern Rumelia, and wrong-footed France over Egypt, by negotiating with the sultan the terms for a British evacuation. On top of that Britain had made an alliance with Austria–Hungary and Italy in 1887, with Bismarck's blessing, that remained the basis of British foreign policy for the following decade.

5

Conclusion

By 1885 Britain's position as a European power had changed dramatically from what it had been in 1815 or even in Palmerston's heyday. His critics (such as Chamberlain and Porter) insist that Britain's influence in European affairs was, in any event, never as great as Palmerston liked to pretend, as in the case of Italian unification. The creation of a united Germany under Prussia (noted for its militarism) inevitably reduced British influence in continental politics even if few anticipated this at the time. The emergence of a strong state in central Europe, reinforced by Bismarck's *Mitteleuropa* alliance system, linked also to Russia, left Britain little room for manoeuvre, as Disraeli was quick to realize, except in matters affecting the Ottoman Empire. The advantages which Britain had seemed to possess as an island power with a strong navy were also diminished when railways gave rapid mobility to land-based forces, as shown in 1866.

The seventy years that followed the battle of Waterloo saw so many changes both in Britain and in much of Europe that the world of 1885 scarcely resembled that of 1815. In many states, especially in western Europe, the growth of towns, the development of railways, and the expansion of trade and manufacturing would be the most obvious signs of 'modernity', matched by the sight of steam ships crowding the ports and harbours along the European coastline. If the 'ironclad' or iron warship had

88

replaced the traditional wooden hulls and sails of the days of Trafalgar, the muskets fired at the battle of Waterloo had been superseded by the breech-loading rifle. The Vienna Settlement itself remained little more than a memory. After withstanding most of the efforts over forty years to modify it in detail, it succumbed to the assault of French and Prussian military force. The Crimean war had ended the consensus amongst the great powers that peace and stability were more important than territorial ambitions and glory. The Concert of Europe was not dead, but its scope seemed limited to issues such as the Eastern Question.

For much of this period Britons had basked in the belief, or illusion, that they were the 'Top Nation'. Not only had Britain defeated Napoleon (single-handedly) at Waterloo, seemingly without regard to the military successes of the allied armies from 1812 onwards, but she had also destroyed the fleets of her main rivals. Add to this heady roll of honour the advantageous, if less glamorous, title of 'First Industrial Nation' and it becomes obvious that Britain enjoyed a unique position in the world for much of the nineteenth century. At least, this was what public opinion was encouraged to believe by Palmerston. He chose to foster the notion of the benevolence of British influence – over the continent and subsequently over the world, extended to include British rule and British power. In such scenarios, 'John Bull' was not only a force to be reckoned with but one to be envied and admired, as he selflessly guided Europeans and other lesser mortals towards the twin benefits of constitutional government and free trade.

Although Disraeli can be seen as following in the footsteps of Palmerston, Gladstone – with his emphasis on the need for morality in international affairs, exercised through the Concert of Europe – clearly stood for a very different tradition in British foreign policy. Aberdeen's conciliatory nature predisposed him to adopt a 'European' viewpoint, which Castlereagh had acquired through personal experience of cooperating with allies for the common good. If changes took place in British foreign policy from 1815 to 1885, they were seemingly not the result of party politics. Aberdeen expressed the view in 1852 that 'the principles of the foreign policy of the country have, for the last thirty years, been the same', despite possible differences in execution. In many ways the most striking change in British policy took place between 1864 and 1874, when both Conservative and Liberal governments shied away from intervention in continental affairs.

The decline of the Concert inevitably reduced Britain's influence in continental affairs. Apart from situations where naval action could be effective, her ability to play an important role in Europe had depended since 1815 on the readiness of the other great powers to resolve their differences or solve problems that arose through conference diplomacy. It was this spirit that Napoleon III had attempted to revive in 1863 in proposing a congress to review the 1815 treaties, partly for the sake of the Poles and the Danes, only to receive an unduly acerbic snub from Earl Russell. His reply that such a meeting would cause 'more apprehension than confidence' was deemed 'deplorable' by the Dutch queen, who described it as 'the death blow of an alliance which ought to have . . . managed the affairs of the Continent, and secured us an era of peace' (19, p. 309). The only conference (unrelated to the Eastern Question or Africa) that did meet, to deal with the crisis over Luxembourg in 1867, was little more than a face-saving affair and even then the role played by the British foreign secretary was less than impressive.

The alternative option for Britain was a strong alliance with France. The combination of the French army and the British navy, reinforced by Britain's economic and financial strength, would have represented a powerful force for peace and a deterrent to the ambitious plans of states such as Prussia, which threatened the stability of Europe in the 1860s. On its own, the British army was obviously incapable of effective intervention on the continent. British indifference to the fate of France in 1870–1 resulted in Britain being virtually alone and isolated, except in matters relating to Turkey in the 1870s. France's subsequent alienation over Egypt after 1882 made Britain over-reliant on German goodwill. A consequence of all this was the dramatic discovery in 1885 that Britain's intended riposte to the new crisis with Russia over Afghanistan of 'forcing the Straits' was barred by the combined opposition of the other powers.

In contrast to her declining influence in Europe, Victorian Britain became 'a world power of the first rank', as even the sceptical Chamberlain concedes. The expansion of her overseas empire put Britain in a unique position amongst the European great powers, even if her rivals were by 1885 also asserting claims to colonies in Africa or Asia. The reasons for her global preeminence seem clear enough. In Kennedy's view, for well over fifty years after 1815, 'This relatively stable international scene allowed the British Empire to rise to its zenith as a global power, in naval and colonial and commercial terms' (**8**, p. XIX). As the chief beneficiary of this period of peace and stability after the Vienna settlement, Britain was almost unchallenged by mid-century in terms of manufacturing capacity and mining. She was also well placed to take advantage of changes that were making western Europe the focus of a global economy in terms of trade and finance.

An important factor in the development of Britain as 'a different type of power from the rest' was that economic wealth was not translated into military power. Spending on defence was deliberately kept down at about £15 million a year in the 1840s, rising to about £27 million in the 1860s, when GNP (gross national product) amounted to one billion pounds. If the armed forces consumed about two or three per cent of GNP (out of a total government expenditure of under ten per cent) this was an almost absurdly low level for a great power with interests in Europe and commitments overseas. It represented a lower proportion than in the eighteenth century (**8**, p. 196). To the Victorians, free trade and economic expansion evidently seemed more fitting objectives than military power, which involved 'unproductive' expenditure. Hence the paradox that Britain was, despite her wealth, relatively weaker in military and diplomatic terms in 1865 or 1885 than she had been in 1815, as regards her standing in Europe. In Africa or Asia, of course, Gatling guns and iron clads continued to demonstrate the superiority of western technology. Two questions arise from this. Firstly, did the concentration of Britain's military effort on the empire lead directly to a major loss of influence in Europe? Secondly, did the emphasis on the virtues of sea power breed 'a sense of isolation from Continental problems'? (**39**; **14**, p. 8)

Many historians, attributing this position to Britain's industrial lead and her naval supremacy, regard this phase of the 'Pax Britannica' as a 'brief and exceptional situation', as Chamberlain calls it. They see the causes of Britain's decline before the end of the century in the failure of British industry to maintain its technological lead over its rivals, especially Germany.

A contemporary observer, Lord Selborne, however, argued

that Britain's greatness rested on the twin pillars of her Navy and her Credit. The wealth derived from overseas investments by the 1880s was unparalleled. It was also augmented by the 'invisible earnings' derived from other financial dealings (short term credit), insurance, shipping, and the myriad of activities provided by the City. Cain and Hopkins' study of the pivotal role of the service sector (as opposed to manufacturing) in the growth of the Victorian economy therefore provides a different perspective on the 'decline' of British power. They suggest that the extension of Britain's global commercial and financial influence implies a large growth in British power after 1850 (5, p. 472). In the late Victorian period, therefore, Britain's standing as an international power was far from being on the wane. With her empire and her world wide commitments her status was unique, so that even as late as 1914 she could still be described as a dynamic power.

Select bibliography*

The literature on foreign affairs is very variable in its useful-
ness, especially to students with a limited amount of time for
reading, so short relevant articles from *Modern History Review*
(1989–97) are listed at the end. Three books stand out as brief,
informative, and very readable works on foreign policy and
European affairs:

1 C. J. Bartlett, *Defence and diplomacy. Britain and the great
   powers, 1815–1914* (Manchester, 1993)
2 A. Sked (ed.), *Europe's Balance of Power, 1815–1848*
   (London, 1979) For references to 2A–D see p. 95.
3 K. M. Wilson (ed.), *British Foreign Secretaries and Foreign
   Policy. From Crimean War to First World War* (London,
   1987) For references to 3A–B see p. 95.

Brief but useful introductions to European affairs, the main
context for British policy in the period to 1885 are:

S. J. Lee, *Aspects of European History, 1789–1980* (London,
1982) chs 5–10
M. S. Anderson, *The Ascendancy of Europe, 1815–1914*
(London, 1985, 2nd edn) chs 1, 2 and 4

*Unnumbered titles refer to books and articles not mentioned
in the text

R. Gildea, *Barricades and Borders, Europe 1800–1914* (Oxford, 1987) chs 3,4, and 7

On British imperialism, the first title listed has become a classic. The second is a new and important, but complex, study of the growth of empire; the other two contain much of interest in an easier format:

4 R. Robinson and J. Gallagher, *Africa and the Victorians* (London, 1961) chs I, III, IV, V
5 P. J. Cain and A. G. Hopkins, *British Imperialism, 1688–1914* (London, 1993) chs 3, 9 (pp. 276–84) 11 (pp. 362–9)
6 B. Porter, *The Lion's Share. A Short History of British Imperialism, 1850–1970* (London, 1975) chs 1–3, pp. 1–97
7 C. C. Eldridge (ed.), *British Imperialism in the Nineteenth Century* (London, 1984) chs 1 and 8

The link between economic growth and military power is well discussed by:

8 P. Kennedy, *The Rise and Fall of the Great Powers* (London, 1988) Fontana edn 1989, ch. 4, pp. 183–248
9 B. Porter, *Britain, Europe and the World, 1850–1982 Delusions of grandeur* (London, 1983)

Three sources that focus on international relations are:

10 F. R. Bridge and R. Bullen, *The Great Powers and the European States System, 1815–1914* (London, 1980)
J. C. Lowe, *The Concert of Europe, 1814–70* (London, 1990)
11 G. Craig, 'The System of Alliances and the Balance of Power', ch. X of *The New Cambridge Modern History* vol X 1830–70, edited by J. P. T. Bury, (Cambridge, 1964)

As regards British foreign policy specifically:

12 M. E. Chamberlain, '*Pax Britannica'? British Foreign Policy 1789–1914* (London, 1988)
13 K. Bourne, *The Foreign Policy of Victorian England, 1830–1902* (Oxford, 1970)

are both useful, but the former although stimulating is too argumentative and too confusing to serve as a good introduction, despite its brevity (180 pages). The latter is a fuller, more straightforward account.

A good brief discussion of British policy 1815–48 is the contribution to Sked (2) by Bartlett (2A). For the Vienna Settlement, the Congress System, and Iberian politics see the other essays in Sked by Dakin (2B) Bridge (2C) and Bullen (2D) respectively.

For the period after 1856, some of the essays on British foreign secretaries edited by Wilson (3) are invaluable, especially Steele's (3A) on Palmerston and Ramm's (3B) on Granville & Gladstone.

Classic texts have their uses but more recent and more accessible works are:

14 C. J. Lowe, *The Reluctant Imperialists. British Foreign Policy, 1878–1902* (London, 1967) chs I–IV
15 P. Lowe, *Britain in the Far East, 1819 to the Present* (London, 1981) pp. 8–18; 34–9
16 R. Millman, *British Foreign Policy and the coming of the Franco-Prussian War* (Oxford, 1965)

The classic texts on British foreign policy are:

17 C. K. Webster, *The Foreign Policy of Castlereagh, 1815–22* (London, 1925) and reprints
18 C. K. Webster, *The Foreign Policy of Palmerston, 1830–41* (London, 1951) 2 vols.
   H. W. V. Temperley, *The Foreign Policy of Canning, 1822–27* (London, 1925)
   A. W. Ward and G. P. Gooch (eds), *The Cambridge History of British Foreign Policy, vol II, 1815–66* (Cambridge, 1923)

Two useful volumes from the Oxford History of England are:

19 E. L. Woodward, *The Age of Reform, 1815–1870* (Oxford, 1938) chs I–IV of Book II are informative
20 R. C. K. Ensor, *England 1870–1914*, (Oxford, 1936)

Biographies of statesmen, full of fascinating trivia, can be a trap for the unwary student, but three clear, readable and reasonably concise works are:

21 M. E. Chamberlain, *Lord Palmerston* (Cardiff, 1987)
22 P. J. V. Rolo, *George Canning* (London, 1965)
   C. J. Bartlett, *Castlereagh* (London, 1966)

Longer, more diffuse, but interesting biographies are:

23 W. Hinde, *George Canning* (London, 1973)
    J. Ridley, *Lord Palmerston* (London, 1970)
24 M. E. Chamberlain, *Lord Aberdeen* (London, 1983)
    K. Bourne, *Palmerston: the Early Years 1784–1841*
    (London, 1982)
25 R. Blake, Lord, *Disraeli* (London, 1966) pbk edn 1969

The last title has useful chapters (XXV-XXVIII) on foreign and imperial affairs 1874–80. There is nothing comparable on Gladstone.

Two contrasting interpretations (the former controversial) of the events leading to war in 1854 are:

26 N. Rich, *Why the Crimean War?* (Hanover, USA, 1985)
27 J. B. Conacher, *The Aberdeen Coalition, 1852–1855* (Cambridge, 1968) pp. 137–260

The remaining titles represent a selection of books that relate, in whole or in part, to some aspect of British foreign policy in the nineteenth century.

28 C. J. Bartlett, *Great Britain and Sea Power, 1815–1853* (Oxford, 1963)
29 C. Howard, *Britain and the Casus Belli, 1822–1902* (London, 1974)
30 P. Kennedy, *The Realities Behind Diplomacy, 1865–1980* (London, 1981) Fontana pp. 17–97
31 P. Kennedy, *The Rise of the Anglo-German Antagonism, 1860–1914* (London, 1980) chs 1, 2, 7, 9 and 10
32 C. R. Middleton, *The Administration of British foreign policy, 1782–1846* (Durham, N.C., 1977)
    D. C. M. Platt, *Finance, Trade and Politics in British Foreign Policy, 1815–1914* (Oxford, 1968)
    W. E. Mosse, *The European Powers and the German Question, 1848–1871* (Cambridge, 1958)
    J. A. S. Grenville, *Europe Reshaped, 1848–78* (London, 1976) Fontana series
    W. N. Medlicott, *The Congress of Berlin and after* (London, 1938)
33 A. J. P. Taylor, *The Struggle for Mastery in Europe, 1848–1914* (Oxford, 1954)

The leading historical journals, while rich in articles on imperialism, are disappointing on British foreign policy. A notable exception is:

34 Loyal Cowles, 'The Failure to Restrain Russia. Canning, Nesselrode and the Greek Question 1825–7', *International History Review*, 1990, vol. 12, pp. 688–720

By contrast, the *Modern History Review* boasts numerous articles, 'themes', and other brief items as shown below, divided into two categories:

Select List of Relevant Articles

Castlereagh's Foreign Policy (Europe After Napoleon)

John Derry	vol. 4	no. 3	Feb. 93

35 George Canning: a Career Blighted by Ambition?

Wendy Hinde	vol. 2	no. 4	Apr. 91

36 The Vienna Settlement ('A Just Equilibrium')

Tim Chapman	vol. 8	issue 1	Sep. 96

The Struggle for Greek Independence

R. Clogg	vol. 5	no. 4	Apr. 94

37 The Crimean War: An Historical Illusion?

Andrew Lambert	vol. 3	no. 2	Nov. 91

Conflict in the Balkans 1876–78

John Morison	vol. 3	no. 1	Sep. 91

The Balance of Power in 1815

P. Catterall and P. Romero	vol. 6	no. 1	Sep. 94
in 1878		no. 2	Nov. 94

38 Palmerston

G. D. Goodlad	vol. 8	issue 1	Sep. 96

Palmerston as Prime Minister

Paul Smith	vol. 4	no. 4	Apr. 93

Select List of Useful Articles

39 Pax Britannica

Muriel Chamberlain	vol. 8	issue 2	Nov. 96

Disraeli

T.A. Jenkins	vol. 8	issue 3	Feb. 97

Napoleon III's Foreign Policy
Tim Chapman   as above
The British Idea of Empire
K. Tidrick   vol. 4   no. 1   Sep. 92
Guardians of Empire
K. Surridge   vol. 7   no. 4   Apr. 96
European Imperialism in the late nineteenth century
Andrew Porter   vol. 2   no. 4   Apr. 91
Britain's 'Decline'
David Reynolds   vol. 4   no. 3   Feb. 93